Bringing Courage to the Courageous

One Chaplain's Journey Across
the Battlefields of Afghanistan

By Chaplain (Captain) Don Williamson,
United States Army

Forward by Chaplain (Brigadier General) (retired)
James Hutchens, author of *Beyond Combat*

xulon
PRESS

18 Feb 2015

Jo,

I pray your continued desire
to serve the Lord leads you to
the Chaplaincy. Never forget
that God is an ever present help
in times of trouble.

Be Strong & courageous

Chaplain Don

Colossians 2: 2-3

For Chaplain Chris Wisdom, my father in the faith, who brought me to Christ over twenty years ago in Basic Training. If not for him, these pages could never have been written, for my spiritual journey may never have begun, and another would have been called to take my place on this mission field.

CONTENTS

Acknowledgments

"I thank my God every time I remember you." (Philippians 1:3)

This book has been nearly two years in the making, and through it all, I am deeply grateful to so many who have helped me complete it. This book was primarily a collection of emails sent to hundreds of friends and family members during my time in Afghanistan. I offer my deepest thanks first and foremost to them — those who faithfully followed the journey of this battalion chaplain, who prayed without ceasing for the safety of our mighty warriors, and who showed their undying support of our mission by sending letters from home, phone cards so we could call home, children's books to read as bedtime stories to our sons and daughters miles away from us, and care packages so we could have a little bit of home while on the battlefield.

To the Command and Staff of the 4th Battalion, 319th Airborne Field Artillery Regiment, I express my deepest thanks for making my first assignment as a battalion chaplain the best I could ever ask for. Lieutenant Colonel Maranian, thank you for your leadership and guidance. For your grace when I made mistakes and your understanding when I gave you counsel. You were a great commander and an even better friend.

Of the many chaplains who gave encouragement and direction, I want to especially thank Chaplain (Colonel) David Smith for his spiritual mentoring, pastoring, and continued guidance as my senior chaplain, Chaplain (Colonel) John Reed for his gentle leading into ministry, and Chaplain (Major) Lee Nelson, my brigade chaplain in the 173rd, who took it upon himself to be a faithful Paul to a young Timothy in a combat zone.

To Barb Beyer for proofreading and editing the final manuscript and her encouragement to actually publish it. Also for the staff at Officers Christian Fellowship for publishing portions of this book in *Command Magazine* and on their website. Fellow author and former marine, Tom Neven, for directing me in the best path to take to get this book into the right hands so many would read it and find hope in this long war.

More importantly, I could never write, preach, or counsel as a chaplain in the Army without my wife Sue's incredible love and support. Your patience is greatly appreciated as well as your ability to "be content in all circumstances" (Philippians 4:11). Thanks for being my best friend and soulmate. I love you more than words can say.

Rachel, Keziah, Hannah and Abigail, you are the greatest blessings in the world! Thanks for letting me grow up as a father as you have grown up as my daughters and for reminding me daily of God's unconditional love and grace for all of His children. I am forever enriched by your lives and your love!

To all those who have touched my life in significant ways, your names may not be mentioned in this book, but you know who you are, and I thank you.

Above all else, I give my greatest appreciation to my Lord and Savior Jesus Christ who has given me abundant life, "redeeming me from the pit and who crowns me with love and compassion." (Psalm 103:4). I stand in awe of your grace and mercy in my life and will forever remain in wonder of what you have done in me and through me.

Forward

*"Now I knew by what I had witnessed that the Living God
still reveals Himself to men who truly seek him."*
~ *Chaplain (Brigadier General) James Hutchens*

*B*ringing Courage to the Courageous is Chaplain Don Williamson's
hands-on and inspiring account of his fifteen-month ministry with his unit in the 173rd Airborne Brigade assigned to
Afghanistan. It is a reminder of why it is so important that
our men and women in uniform, especially in combat, have
chaplains who are competent Soldiers as well as committed
representatives of their faith group, to minister to the deepest
spiritual needs of those in "harm's way." It is also a solemn
reminder of why loved ones left behind will stand for nothing
less.

Having served as a chaplain with the 173rd in Vietnam
I was first struck with Chaplain Williamson's name. You see,
the name of the Commanding General who first took the
173rd to Vietnam in 1965 was Brigadier General Ellis (Butch)
Williamson. Somehow I know General Williamson, now with
the Lord, is pleased to know that Chaplain Williamson has carried on the rich spiritual legacy of the Williamson's.

Chaplain Williamson's experience with the Navigators
at West Point, and his years as a Young Life leader prepared
him well "to earn the right to be heard" as a chaplain. While a

chaplain is assigned to a unit, his/her ministry will only be as effective as his "contact work" and his relationship building with those in his/her unit. Only as those in his unit see him as "the real stuff" does he "earn the right to be heard." Chaplain Williamson has raised the bar by showing how it's supposed to be done.

Chapter 9 on *The Combat Multiplying Chaplain* was especially insightful and should be a part of the curriculum at the Chaplain's School. The chaplain is uniquely qualified to bring prayer based on the Scriptures to bear on the unending challenges faced in a combat situation. Like so many of us who have faced the fears and uncertainties of combat, The Soldier's Psalm, Psalm 91, will be in our mental hard drive forever. That was true of Chaplain Williamson who made Psalm 91 come alive for those in his unit.

The 4th Battalion of the 319th Airborne Field Artillery Regiment of the 173rd Airborne Brigade suffered no casualties during the fifteen months Chaplain Williamson served with this unit. Certainly God is sovereign over matters of life and death, but I must believe that in the Lord's providence he blessed the "ministry of presence" of Chaplain Don Williamson by granting, by His grace, a casualty-free tour of duty.

By Chaplain (Brigadier General) James Hutchens
US Army, Retired
Author of *Beyond Combat*

Introduction

Remember and Do Not Forget

"I always thank my God as I remember you in my prayers"
(Philemon 1:4)

I wear a black bracelet on my right wrist. Nothing flashy, just a black band one-half inch wide with silver lettering. It says simply, "SPC Ryan J. Connolly, A Co, 173rd STB, 173rd ABCT KIA: 24 June 2008." And while it's a reminder of my friend that I lost on the battlefields of Afghanistan, it's also a reminder of so much more. For fifteen months in Afghanistan, I was the battalion chaplain for the 4th Battalion, 319th Airborne Artillery Regiment — the "Big Guns" for the 173rd Airborne Brigade Combat Team (ABCT). For fifteen months, I traveled across the N2KL (Nuristan, Nangahar, Kunar and Locar) Provinces of Afghanistan. For fifteen months, I ministered to our boys on the gunlines at Forward Operating Bases (FOBs) with names like Kalagush and Methar Lam, and Combat Outposts (COPs) with names like Blessing, Lybert and Bella. I had the privilege of ministering to the warriors of the 173rd ABCT — bringing courage to the courageous. And for fifteen months, our battalion never lost a single Soldier to either WIA or KIA, nicknaming us the "Miracle Battalion."

The bracelet also reminds me of my fellow warrior chaplains who stood with me to bring hope to these Paratroopers. It reminds me that of the forty-two Paratroopers who lost their lives fighting for freedom, the 2nd Battalion, 503rd Infantry lost the most. And of my friend, CH (MAJ) Dave Schnarr, who endured 24 Memorial Ceremonies. His unit lost the most, my unit lost none.

Finally, the bracelet reminds me that we are all brothers in arms. We all wear the Winged Bayonet combat patch on our right shoulder. We all fought together. We all served with "The Herd" — Sky Soldiers, Airborne.

And so this is the story of one chaplain's journey on the battlefields of Afghanistan. A journey which brought me, at times, to the very gates of hell, yet never doubting for a moment, that this is what God had been preparing me for my entire life.

I wear a black bracelet to remember, and never forget. . . .

Chapter One

From a Simple Calling . . .

"Therefore, brothers, be all the more diligent to make your calling and election sure." (Acts 1:8b)

In the book, *Taliban*, author Ahmed Rashid interviewed a mullah who said that when Allah had finished creating the world, he took the rest that was left over, and created Afghanistan! The truth of that statement hit me as strongly as the hot air that slammed into me the moment I walked off the C5 at Bagram Air Base in Afghanistan in May 2007. As I walked along the tarmac with the rest of the Paratroopers of the 173rd ABCT, I looked around at the mountains encircling the air base. Much of the scenery reminded me of Missoula, Montana. Snow capped mountains and beautiful trees; this would be my home for the next fifteen months. From the airfield, it was hard to imagine this as a combat zone or that after eighteen years of running from my calling, I was actually standing there at all . . .

Answering the Call

I once heard a pastor say that a calling is simply something that keeps calling you. No matter what you do, you can't shake it. Maybe you are called to be an electrician. Every time you walk into a Lowe's or a Home Depot, you immediately gravitate to the electrical section complete with switches, wires and every type of hanging lamp you can imagine. Others are called to be chefs. Each time you walk into a Barnes and Nobles you gravitate to the cookbook section. You download the latest menus from chef.com, and your favorite show on television is Iron Chef, or Hell's Kitchen.

For me, the calling has always been to ministry. It began when I first became a Christian in 1988 in Basic Training. A man by the name of Chaplain Chris Wisdom led me to the Lord. Having grown up in a church-going home, I first went to chapel, like most privates, because it was the one place where people weren't yelling at you! But every Sunday, I remember sitting in the pew of our World War II cantonment chapel listening to CH Wisdom preach, talking about Jesus in a way I had never heard before. And by the end of basic training, I knew I wanted what he had; I wanted Jesus Christ to be the Lord of my life and I wanted to serve Him always.

From there, I went on to West Point where I was discipled by missionaries with the Navigators Ministry and also got involved in a ministry called Young Life. After my active duty time as a Military Police officer, I became an Area Director with Young Life, ministering to high school and middle school kids for nine years. But I continued to stay in the military reserves and, when 9/11 happened, I eventually found myself deployed to Iraq in support of Operation Iraqi Freedom. And while my job was to be a Battle Captain for the Mine Explosive Ordnance Information Coordination Cell (MEOICC), my *real* job came when I became the worship leader for the little chapel at Camp Victory in Baghdad. For it was there that I met CH (LTC) John Read and sensed the calling to become a chaplain.

The calling to become a chaplain was not something new for me. Were I honest with myself, it was always something that remained in the back of my mind. So when I walked into CH Read's office at Camp Victory one Sunday afternoon, I hadn't been there more than five minutes when I broke down and started crying.

Through my tears, I said to him, "Sir, I think God is calling me to become a chaplain."

Puzzled, he smiled and replied, "Well, why are you crying about that? I think that is a great thing!"

I had no answer.

CH Read sat back in his chair and then poignantly asked, "Don, you've been a missionary with Young Life for what, nine years now?" I looked up at him and nodded.

"And if you were to become a chaplain, what would you do differently?"

"That's just it, sir," I answered reaching for a Kleenex. "I don't think I would do anything differently. I believe that being a chaplain is all about building relationships and earning the right to be heard by Soldiers in the hopes that one day you can get the chance to share the gospel with them. It's the same thing that I do right now in Young Life."

CH Read smiled. "Exactly," he said. "And I wouldn't expect you to do anything different. So I think the real reason why you are crying is because for the last nine years, you have been doing professional ministry with Young Life. It's what you know. Now God is calling you out of your comfort zone, into a new profession. And you are scared at what lies ahead."

In my heart, I knew he was right. So I committed myself right then and there to finish seminary and become a chaplain.

Once I had only about one semester left until my seminary degree would be complete, I called a recruiter out of the 6th Recruiting Training Brigade in Las Vegas, NV in May of 2006. CH (MAJ) Brian Harki was the first to get me started with my Chaplain Candidate Packet. And while I met all the qualifications, it seemed like my desire to become an Active Duty chaplain would not happen. CH Harki let me know that I could not have more than ten years active federal service time prior to becoming a chaplain. When we looked at my DD214

(Certificate of Release from Service) it showed that, because of my recent twelve month deployment to Iraq in Operation Iraqi Freedom II from 2004-2005, I had 10 years, 7 months and 7 days of active service.

Convinced that God was calling me onto active duty, I asked if I could submit a waiver. CH Harki let me know that, while there was no such thing as an active federal service waiver, he would not stop me from submitting one. My wife, Sue, and I wrote the waiver and prayed over it to be approved. We asked several of our friends who had come to be prayer warriors in our lives to pray with us. I contacted my mentor and father in the faith, CH Wisdom, who was working up at the Chief of Chaplains Office at the time to have him pray. We sent off the memorandum and waited.

Miraculously, two weeks later we received word back that, while the waiver was not approved, it no longer mattered because the Army, due to its need to fill many chaplain vacancies, had changed the policy. Now it was possible to have up to fifteen years active federal service and still come on active duty as a chaplain. Sue and I laughed because we had been asking for a waiver, and God changed the Army's policy instead! It seemed like my dream and my calling to go on active duty was about to come true.

But not quite. Army regulations stipulate that a chaplain candidate must have two years prior pastoral experience in a church setting before becoming a chaplain. While this is waiverable, the denomination that agrees to endorse the candidate must write an exception to policy memorandum stating that they think the candidate has met the criteria outside of a church setting. Such was the case for me.

Even though I had been a missionary with Young Life for nine years, this did not, in the Army's eyes qualify as pastoral experience. Despite me trying to tell CH Harki that my job as an area director had many identical responsibilities as that of a church senior pastor, he still said that I needed a waiver.

Thankfully, my endorsing agency, the Evangelical Church Alliance (ECA), was more than happy to write the exception to policy. After receiving the exception to policy from the ECA, CH Harki called to tell me that my packet was finally ready to go before the board.

"But I have to tell you, Don," he explained. "There is a requirement now that twenty percent of all candidates who go before the board that request active duty will get chosen, instead for the Army Reserves. And one of the deciding factors always is the pastoral experience waiver."

Inwardly enraged at this revelation, but trying to keep my cool, I calmly said, "Let me get this straight, sir. You mean to tell me that there is a good chance that because I have not served on a church staff for two years but rather have been a missionary for nine years, that doesn't matter? In fact, even though I am a prior service Army officer, there is a chance that I could get beat out for an active duty slot by a young pastor, even though he has never once served in the military, simply because he has been on a church staff?"

"That's what I'm telling you, Don," he said with no emotion through the phone.

"Ok," I said sounding defeated. "I guess we'll just have to see." I calmly said goodbye, but after hanging up the phone that was when me and God went at it! The whole ride home from work in the car, I was screaming at God.

"Do you not know how hard of a decision this has been, Lord?!" I yelled into the air, pounding my fists on the steering wheel. "Is this what you have brought me to?! You put this calling in my heart only to let me know that the best I can hope for is reserve duty?"

I continued to rant and rave. At each stop light, I'm sure that people in the cars next to me were wondering if they were watching road rage in action! As I rounded the hill to my home in Missoula, Montana, I was finally quiet.

In my spirit, I heard the Lord ask, "Are you finished?"

Defeated, I sighed and said, "Yes, Lord. I can't make my case any stronger with you, and I'm tired of trying to make this happen for me."

Then immediately, the Lord brought me to the passage in 1 Samuel 16 where Samuel had gone to Jesse's house because the Lord had sent him there to anoint a new king. When the first of Jesse's sons came through the door, Samuel said, "Surely the Lord's anointed is before him."

> *But the Lord said to Samuel, "Do not look on his appearance on the height of his stature, because I have rejected him. For the Lord sees not as man sees: man looks on the outward appearance, but the Lord looks on the heart." ~ 1 Samuel 16:7 (ESV)*

With that verse still ringing in my ears, I pulled the car over because I was weeping so hard. I lifted up my hands to God and said, "Lord, you know the desire of my heart. You know my desire to be called onto active duty. Yet, it is not my plans that will succeed, but Yours. I trust You in all of this."

From that point on, I placed my calling in the Lord's hands and I waited for the results. Three weeks later, CH Harki called to tell me that I had been accepted as a chaplain and that I was being brought on active duty! The process had been worth it.

The day that I received the phone call was September 29, 2006. Not surprisingly, that same day the devotional reading in Oswald Chamber's *My Utmost for His Highest* had this to say:

> *If a man or woman is called of God, it doesn't matter how difficult the circumstances may be. God orchestrates every force at work for His purpose in the end. If you will agree with God's purpose, He will bring not only your conscious level but also all the deeper levels of your life, which you yourself cannot reach, into perfect harmony.*

When God first called Moses to lead the people of Israel out of bondage in Egypt, he was eighty years old. The first forty years of his life he lived as a member of Pharaoh's family. After murdering a guard, he fled Egypt into the Midian wilderness where he lived for another forty years. But God had him go through both of those events in order to shape who he was and what he was being called to do. The forty years in Pharaoh's court no doubt allowed him to go back there with relative ease and demand the release of God's people. Likewise, the forty years in the wilderness allowed him to lead the children of Israel in their wanderings before entering the promised land.

Although *my* timeline is condensed (eighteen vs. forty years), I believe that the same can be said for me and the journey that God ultimately put me on in becoming a chaplain in the Army. For nine years I was in the active duty Army as both an enlisted infantryman and a military police officer. Additionally, for nine years I was an Area Director for Young Life where I learned how to do relational ministry—going where kids were at, becoming a part of their lives, and earning the right to be heard. Yet both of those things were what God used to shape me and mold me into becoming what He had been preparing me for my whole life.

And So it Began . . .

Between September 2006 and May 2007, my life and that of my family's changed forever. We left our ministry with Young Life in Missoula, Montana and, after 10 weeks at Fort Jackson for Chaplain's Basic Officer Leadership Course, headed over to Bamberg, Germany for my assignment in the 173rd Airborne Brigade Combat Team. Though the Brigade had had a long combat history, fighting in every major conflict since World War II, it had only been reactivated in June 2000. (Additional battalions were activated to "round-up" the 173rd to a full and modernized Brigade Combat Team.) Not surprisingly, the first book I ever read as a chaplain was written by a former

173rd chaplain who served with the brigade in Vietnam. *Beyond Combat*, written by Chaplain Jim Hutchens, tells the story of a chaplain and his adventures with the 173rd in the jungles and rice fields of Vietnam. I remember thinking to myself that if I could be half the chaplain Chaplain Hutchens was in combat, then I will have accomplished something in my calling to serve, and hopefully save for eternity, America's greatest warriors.

Not long into the Basic Course at the Chaplain School, God led me to my theme verse for my upcoming deployment. Joshua 1:9 says, "Have I not commanded you? Be strong and courageous. Do not be terrified; do not be discouraged, for the Lord your God will be with you wherever you go." Knowing the history of the 173rd, I believed that I was about to minister to some of the toughest warriors in the Army. Weren't they already courageous? These warriors, these mighty men and women, what could I bring them that didn't already have? I could bring them courage that they didn't have of their own accord. I could bring them the courage of the Lord. Thus began my motto for my time in the 4-319th— *Bringing Courage to the Courageous.*

My family touched down on German soil April 10, 2007. By May 10, 2007, I would be on a plane heading to Afghanistan. The 173rd had been tasked as part of the President's "surge package" with 5 more brigades heading to Iraq and 1 more heading to Afghanistan. Since the 173rd (or the two infantry battalions, 1st of the 503rd and the 2nd of the 503rd) had experience in Afghanistan when the War on Terror hit back in 2001 and then again in 2005, it seemed the smartest thing for the Department of Defense to send them back there as a whole brigade for Operation Enduring Freedom VIII.

Though I didn't have much chance to get to know the Soldiers in the 4-319th Field Artillery Battalion prior to arriving in country, I *was* able to travel with my battalion commander on the flight over there. A quiet man who stressed the importance of his Soldiers remaining the "quiet professionals," LTC Steve

Maranian took his job as commander of an artillery battalion about to head to war very seriously. Himself a veteran of the Iraq war, LTC Maranian knew what his Brigade Commander would expect out of his "big guns". He also knew the cost.

In one of my conversations with him on the plane ride over, I looked at LTC Maranian and said, "Sir, I know only God can do this, but I am praying for no casualties in our battalion, and that each and every one of our Soldiers returns home to their families safe and sound."

Nodding in agreement, but also realizing that there was a high degree of doubt that could ever happen, he simply replied, "Chaplain, if that happens, I will sleep soundly the rest of my days on this earth."

So would I.

Chapter Two

. . . to a Simple Place Called Kalagush

"And you will be my witnesses in Jerusalem and in all Judea and Samaria, and to the ends of the earth." (Acts 1:8b)

The continuous hum of the Humvee and sweltering heat was making it next to impossible for me to stay awake. Traveling with Golf Battery, the battalion's movement and logistics element, I was in a ten-vehicle convoy heading to Mehtar Lam on what seemed like the only hardball road in all of Afghanistan. Having caught a C-130 cargo plane out of Bagram Airfield with my assistant, SPC Marcus Marshall, we had landed at the brigade headquarters in Jalalabad and hitched a ride with Golf Battery up to Mehtar Lam in the hopes of flying up to FOB Kalagush where the battalion headquarters was.

Renamed from FOB Jalalabad to FOB Fenty shortly after we arrived as a brigade and set up our headquarters, it was named in honor of LTC Joseph J. Fenty, battalion commander for 3rd Squadron, 71st Cavalry Regiment, 10th Mountain Division who had been killed when a Chinook helicopter had crashed shortly after takeoff in 2006. Our original plan was to arrive at Fenty, meet my new brigade chaplain, CH (MAJ) Lee Nelson, then catch a flight on a Chinook to Kalagush the next day. But as I was soon to learn, air assets in theater were always at a premium, and unless a bird was heading where you were going, you needed to quickly look for alternate modes of transportation.

During the fifteen months that our battalion would spend in Afghanistan, Golf Battery would travel close to 250,000 miles in convoys resupplying the battalion. Their mission was one of constant vigilance and mission success. Units in the battalion always needed resupply, and these young mechanics, chemical specialists, fuel handlers and truck drivers, also held jobs as 50-cal machine gunners in Humvee turrets during convoys. Although they would be hit with everything from RPGs to IEDs, the battery never lost a Soldier to a battlefield injury.

When Marshall and I caught word that Golf Battery was heading to FOB Fenty to pick up ammo, we arranged to hitch a ride with them. After gathering all the willing Soldiers around me to pray for safe travels and God's protection, Marshall got into the Convoy NCOIC's (non-commissioned officer in charge) vehicle and I hopped into the Convoy commander's. So began our journey as the Battalion's Circuit Riding Ministry Team!

In a convoy, vehicles don't travel faster than about 35 MPH. This makes for a long trip. What's more, when you are not the gunner up top, the vehicle commander (called the TC), or the driver, there's not much for you to do but just sit and stare out the window. And while the ride itself was decent, the scenery was magnificent. 15,000 foot high mountains set as a backdrop for desert sands. Crystal green rivers rushing through rich marshlands and past simple mud homes.

Looking at the serenity of the scenery, my mind started to wander back home. I thought about what my wife was doing at that moment. I prayed for my daughters as they got ready for school. I was reminded of my last night with them and how

Hannah, my eight year-old had quietly sobbed in my arms as I rocked her to sleep in her bed only to have her say, "OK, I'll see you later daddy," when I finally closed the door. How long fifteen months seemed at that moment!

My daydreaming was interrupted, however, when our 50-cal gunner yelled down from the turret, "Hey sir," he yelled to the convoy commander. "I just thought you should know that there is a white van following us about three hundred meters back and it's been there for about a mile now."

Immediately, the young lieutenant shouted back, "Well if he comes any closer, you light him up!"

Sitting directly behind him, and wanting to make sure I had heard him right, I tapped him on the shoulder and said, "Excuse me lieutenant, what did you just say?"

Almost incredulously, he looked back at me and yelled, "Look chaplain, I know what I'm doing! Just sit back and enjoy the ride and let me deal with what needs to be done with these yayhoos behind us."

Not satisfied, I tapped him on the shoulder again. "Look LT, you may think that I am some brand new chaplain out here in bad guy country," I screamed back over the engine noise. "But I know a thing or two about convoys. Now this young private in the turret here needs a little more clarification on your escalation of force policy don't you think, before you simply have him haul off and fire a 50-cal at a van simply because it is getting closer?"

At that point, I tugged on the private's ACU pant leg to get his attention. "Don't fire," I mouthed, and he nodded in understanding.

Thankfully, the white van turned off onto another side road, and the private gave the all clear.

Shortly after that, the convoy commander looked back at me and yelled, "You're just a chaplain! What the hell do you know about rules of engagement in a convoy?"

I smiled and simply said, "More than you think I do." For the rest of the ride I was in another vehicle, in another convoy, in another war.

A Cloud, A Convoy and A Connection

April 9, 2004. I was the Military Police Officer assigned to the 379th Engineer Battalion out of Missoula, Montana as their Anti-terrorism/Force Protection Officer. Our battalion had been mobilized in support of Operation Iraqi Freedom II to work the Mine Explosive Cell for 3rd Corps in Camp Victory, Iraq. Though the job would eventually entail fourteen-hour days behind a computer screen, the road from Kuwait, where all units came into theater, to Baghdad would be five hundred miles on a two-day convoy. Because of my experience as a military police officer, the battalion commander made me the convoy commander.

In the middle of the night before our departure, I felt someone tapping me on the shoulder while I was asleep. I opened one eye to see one of our young Soldiers, Brian.

"Sir, I'm sorry to wake you, but do you have a minute?" he asked.

"Sure," I said rubbing my eyes to try and focus on him. "What's up?"

"I can't do, it, sir," he said, with tears welling up in his eyes. "I can't do this convoy. I can't stop thinking that one of us isn't going to make it. I've never been so scared, but I don't want anybody else to know that. I don't want other people to think that I'm a coward."

I thought how poignant it was that God would bring this Soldier to me. Earlier that evening, I had called my pastor to ask if he would pray with me. My courage was waning. I thought of my family back home. I wanted to see them again. I thought of all the things that I still wanted to do for the Lord, and yet I was unsure what was ahead of me. I needed to pray with some warriors.

I remember my pastor praying for a hedge of protection around our convoy, and a cloud to go before us that we would be able to testify that our God was with us. We prayed for no injuries and no incidents. We prayed for the supernatural hand of God to lead us north. As I walked back to my tent, I knew that if there were to be no incidents, no small arms fire, no Inderect Exlosive Devices (IEDs), no Rocket Propelled Grenades (RPGs) aimed at us, then it would truly have to be from God and God alone.

So when I looked at this young Soldier now sitting on the edge of my cot, I thought I knew how Jesus must have felt when His disciples were racked with fear because of the storm on the Sea of Galilee. They came to Him, terrified. "Lord, don't you care if we drown?" And He said just what needed to be said at the time, "Where is your faith?" My pastor had strengthened my faith. Now I needed to strengthen Brian's.

"Well, I can guarantee you that there is not a Soldier in this tent who isn't scared," I said in my most reassuring tone. "And the ones that say they aren't are liars. What we are about to do is dangerous, but you need to trust that God is going to protect our convoy."

"But how can you be so sure?" He asked, choking back the tears that seemed to be flowing pretty regularly now. "I mean, anything can happen out there."

"You're right, anything can happen. But that's why I think we should leave it in the Lord's hands, and trust that He knows what He's doing."

This young Soldier looked confused, so I put it straight on the line with him. "Look, you need to know that there are literally thousands of people praying for this unit and for our convoy to Baghdad. People all over the world are praying for us — and I know that God hears those prayers."

I could tell he still had doubts, so all I said to him was, "Trust me, God is real, and after this week, you'll know that He led us the whole way."

I guess what I've realized in that story of Jesus and His disciples, is that we really don't know where they were in their faith. Mark tells us that the disciples looked at each other after Jesus had calmed the storm and "they were more afraid than ever and said to each other, "Who is this? Even the wind and the waves obey Him!"

I put my hand on Brian's shoulder and prayed for him and then I encouraged him to try and get some sleep. As I drifted back off into dreamland, I remember praying, "Oh, God, protect this convoy. I pray for a covering, and I pray that You go before us like You did for Israel, not because of anything we have done, but simply for the sake of Your name."

Just before we began to move, I pulled the whole unit together to pray and to give them a blessing. I read to them Deuteronomy 20:1-4.

> *"When you go to war against your enemies and see horses and chariots and an army greater than yours, do not be afraid of them, because the Lord your God, will be with you. When you are about to go into battle, the priest shall come forward and address the army. He shall say: 'Hear, O Israel, today you are going into battle against your enemies. Do not be fainthearted or afraid; do not be terrified or give panic before them. For the Lord your God is the one who goes before you against your enemies to give you victory.'"*

With that, all of the Soldiers got into their respective vehicles. Drivers checked their maps, TCs got one last commo (short for communications) check, and gunners got behind the crew served weapon (either a MK-19 grenade launcher or a 50-cal machine gun) atop the vehicle. I took one last look over our small, yet lethal, convoy before getting into my own vehicle strategically placed in the middle of the convoy. I prayed, "Lord, I am the convoy commander. These men are my responsibility. Grant me the wisdom to make split second decisions when I have to, to be calm in the midst of chaos. Give me the strength that comes only from Your power, that I may give these men and women strength. Guide this convoy. I trust in only You." I got into my vehicle and got on the radio, "Hotel 2-5 this is Hotel 2-1, you are clear to move." An hour later, we crossed the border into Iraq. We put magazines in our weapons and began scanning our sectors. "This is Hotel 2-1, welcome to Iraq." Our journey north had begun.

The first half of our convoy was, as expected, uneventful. Not much enemy activity has happened in southern Iraq since March of 2003 when the war began. As the coalition forces pushed the Iraqi army back north to Baghdad, most of the cities experienced relative peace. They have even begun to express their newfound freedoms by conducting (mostly) peaceful rallies and demonstrations. The southern people of Iraq are predominantly Shi'ia Muslim and have, for the last thirty-six years, been oppressed by the Sunni minority found in the Baathist Party.

The lull in the action gave me the chance to take some pictures and to take in the country where I was to live for the next year. Right from the moment we crossed the border, I witnessed the absolute poverty of these people. I struggled knowing that I was headed to a camp that was one of Saddam's ninety-three palaces and all around me were mud homes no bigger than a one car garage. In every town, children ran out to wave at us. Some men held bottles up begging for clean water. Others yelled obscenities at us. Most were just trying to make some money to feed their families. This was the area that used to be known as the "marsh" farmers. Eighty percent of the people in this region made their living farming salt in the rich marshes. But in 1995, Saddam instituted a "marsh reclamation" project, drying up ninety percent of all the wetlands. He believed all of the Shiites in the south were against him and his regime, so he dried up the marshes to force them to leave. Many did not leave. Instead, they stayed because this was their home, and they tried to make a living some other way. As we drove through bazaars literally on the shoulders of their four lane highway, people were selling everything from soda pop to gasoline.

As we neared the first camp where we would stay the night before pushing north, a squadron of Apache Gunships flew alongside our convoy for about the last half hour of the trip. My thoughts went to Psalm 91. It has been given to Soldiers for years as the "Soldier's psalm." "For He orders his angels to protect you wherever you go." (Psalm 91:11). He had surely done that. Our first leg was complete.

Unexpectedly, however, we got held up at that camp for nearly five days. Insurgents had blown three overpasses and two bridges. The safest route north was not trafficable until the engineers could repair the damage. During our travels earlier that day, I had made the decision to have our gunships cover the overpasses as the rest of the convoy traveled underneath them. Each time, the overpasses were empty with no threat around. Many times I fought the urge to come on the radio and tell them that they didn't need to cover the next one because the threat didn't seem to be there. "No," I thought, "This is good training. We need to keep doing this for when we move closer to the city." When I heard that the enemy had destroyed those bridges, I was glad that we had "practiced" them when we did.

The break, however, turned out to be a nice stay for me. One of my former Young Life leaders from Lexington, VA, Jake Wilson, a graduate of the Virginia Military Institute, was the night shift officer in charge at Camp Cedar. So we got to spend some good time together. We ate a number of meals together, and we found time to pray for each other. I had to smile when I thought how God had brought the two of us through so much over the years, only to bring us to Iraq at the same time.

But as each day passed and we were prevented from moving north, the situation in theater continued to deteriorate. Every time I would head over to the Movement Control Team (MCT) office for a threat update, it seemed like the fighting was getting worse. Our commander felt that if we waited any longer, it wouldn't help anything, so we made the decision to push north. We told the Soldiers we would be moving in the morning. As I walked by one of the tents, I heard a Soldier say, "We're heading right into a hornet's nest! If we don't get shot at tomorrow, it will be a miracle!"

"You can say that again," I thought to myself. And I prayed that God would make that miracle a reality.

The Covering Cloud

That next day would be a day that I will remember for the rest of my life. Even though it had been over three years since that convoy, I can still recall it like it was yesterday. I remember the traffic on the radio and the bridges we had to diligently cover as we went under them. I remember the thirty miles of dirt road that we had to travel, not being able to see the vehicle in front of you, trusting that your radio would not stop working. But most of all, I remember the haze that surrounded us for two-thirds of the trip.

About ten miles after we left Camp Cedar, a cloudy haze came and literally surrounded our convoy. At first I thought that it was because of the early morning haze, but when it hadn't left by 0930, I began to think otherwise. Could this be the hedge of protection that people were praying for us? Is this the cloud that was going before us? The more I thought about it, the more excited I got. As I moved into a position where I could see the front of the convoy, I noticed that I could see the first vehicle and nothing beyond that. When I asked my driver if she could see the last vehicle, she said, "Yes, sir, but I can't see anything after that." Whenever we covered a bridge and the lead vehicle moved into position to cover, the cloud seemed to close in on the new lead vehicle. I thought of Psalm 105:39 "God hid them under a cloud and guided them by fire during the night."

When we arrived at our second "truck stop" to refuel, I shared that scripture with my friend Mitch. Mitch had just come to know the Lord a couple of months ago. He was traveling in my vehicle and was in charge of all the commo. So he was really excited at that! But when we pulled out, not five miles up the road, Mitch says to me, "Hey Don, where'd the cloud go?! We're about to move into the hottest part of this operation, and the cloud's gone."

He was right. The cloud was not surrounding our vehicles like it had for the last three hours. I turned around and looked at him and said, "Mitch, I'm not sure, but God's brought us this far, He'll lead us the rest of the way, I just know it!" I felt like Caleb when he had returned from the land God was going to give the Israelites. All of the people trembled with fear as news of giants in the land spread throughout the camp, but Caleb silenced the people and said, "We should go up and take possession of the land, for we can certainly do it!" (Numbers 13:30). I wasn't sure how God was going to get us through this unscathed, but I believed He would.

No sooner had I thought that, then a convoy of Military Police Humvees rolled by us. These are the same vehicles that I used to command as an MP. Every one of them was an up-armored vehicle with the MK-19 40mm grenade launcher in the turret. To see a convoy of ten move alongside us was awesome! Knowing how they employ these vehicles, I knew that it was one squad. I wondered what MP platoon had been tasked to patrol this road. They traveled alongside us for about twenty miles, and then, at a turnaround, headed south again; but not before another squad had come up on our right side to travel with us. I wished that I had had communications with them because I wanted to thank them for their escort. They didn't have to do that. Their job was to patrol the whole highway, and yet they stayed right next to us until we exited off into the city. But then I thought of the many who were praying, and I would not have been surprised to hear that one of the many prayer warriors had prayed specifically for an MP escort for us! Angels, wearing MP broussards!

The last thirty minutes of our trip was a whirlwind. Because of the blown bridge, we couldn't enter into the main gate of the camp, so we had to travel right through the heart of the city into the back gate. I closed up the convoy to within fifteen meters of each vehicle and halted all radio traffic except my commands. We were within ten miles of our destination and mission complete, and I needed to have full control of the convoy. Of course, at this point, I was merely a vessel that the Lord was using to bring this convoy safely in.

In the weeks that would follow our convoy in the city, that route would become the heaviest hit route for IED attacks and ambushes on coalition convoys. A number of Soldiers would be wounded, some fatally. But by the grace of God, we experienced none of that. I mean nothing. No IEDs or small arms fire. No complex attacks aimed at small convoys like ours. Not even a kid throwing rocks at us. For the sake of His name, God had led us through it all, and had given us the victory.

The voice of Staff Sergeant (SSG) Peters, our guide from Camp Victory, came over the radio, "On behalf of the 1138th Engineers (the unit we were replacing), I would like to welcome you to Victory Base." The next voice was the battalion commander. "Well done, Hotel 2-1, mission complete."

"Roger, sir, thank you," I said and turned my head to look out the window. The tears filled my eyes as I looked around me. We were inside the walls of Camp Victory. God had done it, just like He said He would, and all I could do was take it all in, praising Him for His sovereign protection of thirty-six Soldiers in a theater of 125,000.

A Connection

As the days passed, we got settled into our small trailers (my space was about six by twelve), got trained up on our specific duties and went to the task we were called here to do for the next year. In that time, our brigade Sergeant Major, CSM Johnson, came up to me and said, "Hey sir, did you know that I got one of your emails?"

I gave him a quizzical look. "You did?" I asked. "Did I send something to you in the last day or so?" For I had only the day before gotten my official email here in theater.

"No, I got it about a week ago. My parents are actively involved in Young Life in South Carolina, and they received the one you sent asking for prayer for your unit as you convoyed north from a friend who had received it from the president, Denny Rydberg. Are you involved with Young Life somehow?"

I laughed and told him that I was the Area Director in Missoula.

"Well, you need to know that you had global coverage on that one. It made it all the way back to me right here in Victory!" he exclaimed.

I thought about the significance of what he had just told me. The sergeant major's office was in the next room from where we would work for the next year. I had asked for prayer that God would lead us right to the gates of Camp Victory. God had done one better; He covered us all the way to the doorstep of our office!

Mehtar Lam, Afghanistan, May 2007

With a smile on my face as I looked out of the window of the uparmored Humvee, remembering how He had protected a little battalion from Montana for fifteen months in Iraq, I wondered to myself, would God do the same thing for our battalion in Afghanistan? Only He could answer that. But as we turned onto the dirt road that led to Mehtar Lam, there was one thing I carried in my heart as this unit's Man of God. By God's grace, I've experienced Him do some amazing things in my life, and in that of my family's life. And though I have never actually heard the audible voice of God, I have always believed that He speaks to me. While I've never been physically healed, I have felt the power of God's healing and seen it happen to my children and to Soldiers around me. And though I've never actually seen God, after what I had experienced in my last deployment, there would never be a doubt in my mind that He is with me — always. It might be in the person next to me, it might be in a child's eyes. It might be in the army of military police that appear out of nowhere. Or it might just be in the cloud that surrounds us and goes before us, to give us victory. So I prayed, "Bring the miracle, O Lord!"

View of FOB Kalagush from one of the guard towers. It would be home to the Headquarters, 4th Battalion, 319th Airborne Field Artillery Regiment (Task Force King) from May 2007-July 2008

Chapter Three

Staying Up Late

*"I will make a covenant of peace with them and drive
away danger from the land.
Then my people will be able to camp safely in the wildest places
and sleep in the woods without fear." (Ezekiel 34:25, NLT)*

I have a confession to make. I don't sleep very well in a single
bed. During the deployment, Sue and I celebrated our fif-
teenth wedding anniversary. Sleeping next to someone that
long, you get used to having them next to you, feeling their
warmth, hearing them breathe, reaching your arm out to hold
them. So when you are away, it's much harder to fall asleep.

As a result, I wake up often, or it takes me a while to drift
off. Most of the time, I try to combat that by watching an
episode of *Monk*, laughing my way through a half-hour of
Everybody Loves Raymond, or simply reading a book. But whenever I am deployed, I've found that if I go out for a little late
night walk, it calms me down enough that I can crawl back
into bed and get some needed rest. I guess I would also say
that being in a combat zone makes it hard to shut your brain
down. There is always the chance of an attack, either direct or
indirect, and if you let your mind wander, no doubt it could
cause many nights of insomnia.

One sweltering night early in June, shortly after arriving to our Battalion headquarters at FOB Kalagush, happened to be one of those nights. It started out great. My daughters had been wondering when I would be able to tell them a bedtime story, so I made sure to stay up a little later than usual in order to call back home and tell them one. Sue put her cell phone on speaker and put it in the middle of the room so the girls could hear the story. And I had a lot of fun telling it. Hannah has often told me that whenever I do that, "It's like you are right here telling it!" But I have to admit, it also made me a little homesick. (Which would be a good reason why I couldn't fall right to sleep.)

So I decided to go for a walk around the FOB. At several locations along the wall, we have guard towers that are manned twenty-four seven. I made my way over to one of them for a visit. As I got closer, one of the guards shined his red lens flashlight at me.

"Who goes there?" he asked.

"It's the chaplain," I responded.

"Oh, hey sir!" the Soldier said, surprised. "What brings you out here so late at night?"

Climbing up the ladder to the tower, I said, "Well, it's a nice night out, so I decided to check up on some of my favorite Soldiers."

Barely able to make out his silhouette in the darkness, I could sense the Soldier didn't quite know how to react to that statement. Then he said matter-of-factly, "Yeah, but sir, we stay up late so you don't have to."

I smiled and clapped my hand onto his armor-vest protected shoulder. "I know buddy." I replied, close enough to see the reflection of the night sky in his eyes. "But it never hurts to get a visit of encouragement, right?"

"You bet, Chaps," he said, obviously appreciative of the company. "It's always good to see you."

For the next ten or fifteen minutes, these two Soldiers and I (there are always two on duty at night at each tower) talked about a myriad of things. I learned that one of them was going home in a few weeks for R&R leave. His baby was not quite a month old when he deployed. I found out that the other was only nineteen years old. He had just been born the year I graduated high school. Man, did I start to feel my age then! Towards the end of our time together, I asked if I could say a quick prayer for them.

"Sure, sir," the guard said. "Always love it when you pray for us."

I put my arms around those two guys and prayed for safety both for their shift and for continued protection over the FOB. I asked that God would be with them throughout the night and help them to stay awake and alert. I prayed for their families. And as always, I prayed that all of us would make it through this deployment safely and return home to the ones we love. We all said, "Amen" and with that, I climbed back down the ladder, and headed towards my hooch.

As I was walking back to my hooch, I was reminded of the famous scene in *A Few Good Men* where Lieutenant Weinberg asked Commander Galloway why she was so adamant about defending two marines who were on trial for killing a fellow marine in a "Code Red" gone bad.

Without hesitation, she wheeled around and looked Lieutenant Weinberg right in the eyes and responded, "Because they stand on a wall each and every night and say, 'Nothing's gonna hurt you tonight, not on my watch.'"

The comment that that young Soldier made, all of nineteen years old, still echoed in my head.

"But sir, we stay up late so you don't have to."

How many times have I heard people back home talk about this generation of kids? How often have people said to me, "These kids don't care about anything. They are so selfish. We've become a society that simply gives kids everything nowadays and places no expectations on them. They'll never amount to anything."

How I wish they could see our Soldiers over here! These young men and women are willing to give the ultimate sacrifice for many in their country who've written them off as selfish, immature leeches of society. These Soldiers often tell me that I give them inspiration, when, in reality, they are the ones who inspire me. They inspire me to be a better chaplain and a better servant. They inspire me to pray for them without ceasing. They inspire me to be a better Soldier.

"We stay up late so you don't have to."

As I crawled into bed and started to drift off to sleep, I thought of the psalmist when he said, "The Lord never slumbers nor sleeps." (Psalm 121:4) And I was grateful for another day to serve the One who protects and cares for these unselfish, untiring, dedicated men and women who protect our freedom.

Chapter Four

Making the Hard Call

"Endure hardship with us like a good Soldier of Christ Jesus." (2 Timothy 2:3)

Early on in the deployment, the Internet in the Morale, Welfare and Recreation (MWR) tent went down for seventy-two hours. Whenever this happens it is usually either (a) because our FOB is under attack and we have sent out the Quick Reaction Force (QRF) and all available Internet assets need to be used for operational purposes, or (b) because there has been engagement somewhere and a unit has experienced a casualty. Consequently, the MWR shuts down the Internet so that no one can get online with instant messaging (IM) or email and notify their loved ones back home about a buddy that may have been injured or killed before the Army has had the chance to officially notify the family. Neither of these are pleasant reasons, and I wish I could say that neither happened, but it did. On June 7, 2007, a patrol from Mehtar Lam (just south of Kalagush) was hit by an IED. Everyone in the vehicle was injured, and one of the Soldiers was killed.

A part of me was able to breathe a "sigh of relief" because even though there were Soldiers from our battalion on the patrol, none of them were in the vehicle that got hit.

So, in some sense, I was thankful that those whom I had been charged to shepherd were all right. But in the whole scheme of things, the loss of any life in war is tragic. For our sister unit in Mehtar Lam, this was the first KIA in their battalion since WWII. A National Guard battalion out of Arizona, the 1-158th Infantry "Bushmasters," were assigned to the Provincial Reconstruction Team (PRT) as their Protective Security Detail (PSD) whenever the team went out on a mission. Their head-quarters was attached to the 173rd as an additional maneuver battalion, though most of their infantry platoons were scattered throughout the northeast of the country performing security for the PRTs. Thankfully, they had a chaplain assigned to them in Mehtar Lam and he began making the arrangements for the memorial ceremony — a crucial element in war where Soldiers in the battalion come together to remember their brother in arms and move forward with the mission.

The chaplain, CH (1LT) Chris Melvin, called me shortly after the incident happened to bounce some ideas off me and get some encouragement for the task at hand. When it looked like much of the battalion, which was scattered throughout the battlefield, would not be able to make it there, I told him I thought maybe we could get the Soldiers that were assigned up here at Kalagush to go down for the ceremony. So I went over to the PRT commanding officer, a Navy Commander, and asked if we could make arrangements for them to go down.

"Sir, do you have a second?" I said approaching entering his office.

"Yeah, Chaps! Come on in and have a seat." Motioning me in, Commander Sam Paparo truly looked the part of a Naval Commander. An F-18 fighter pilot for eighteen years, he had flown combat missions over most of the last major US engagements. Himself a graduate of "Top Gun" at Miramar in California, you got to see why these guys are considered the best of the best.

"Sir, I'm sure you probably already know about what happened near Mehtar Lam today. I wanted to see what we are doing about getting the guys who are from that unit down there for the memorial ceremony," I said waiting to hear him tell me that the arrangements had already been made.

Without hesitation, the Commander said, "Yeah, we're not going to be sending any from the PRT."

I looked at him quizzically. "Excuse me, sir?"

He looked at me with an intensity that said he meant business. "Look, Chaps. It's just too dangerous to send these guys down there. Three months ago, there were guys from a unit heading to a memorial ceremony when their convoy was hit by an IED. Everyone in the vehicle was killed. So I am not about to send these Soldiers to a memorial ceremony and risk their own lives."

He could tell that I didn't like that answer. "Chaps, you have to understand that even though this death is tragic, sometimes the best thing for Soldiers in times of grief is work and getting back out there. I also believe that the guys who were closest to him are already at Mehtar Lam. If we focus too much on this, then morale will begin to cave. I've buried too many of my buddies to know otherwise."

As soon as he finished speaking, I knew that he was right. And I also could see why he was a commander. To be honest, I needed to be reminded of it myself. This was still a war. And wars are awful things. They are the result of a fallen world. And while it is our job as chaplains to honor the dead, it's also our job to nurture the living. Sending the platoon over a route that had been come to be known as "IED alley" would definitely not have been nurturing the living.

That evening, I was reminded of a scene in the movie *U-571* where the captain of the submarine, Lieutenant Commander Mike Dahlgren looked at his executive office, Lieutenant Andrew Tyler, who was upset that he was not getting command of his own ship. The captain looked at him and said, "Can you make the hard call, son? Can you make the decision as to who lives and who dies if it came down to that? You're not ready for command because you are too close to the men."

That Sunday in chapel, Commander Paparo was sitting in the back row of the liturgical service that we had started at Kalagush. He seemed to immerse himself in the whole thing. There was a faith and assurance about this man who truly trusts in the Sovereign God that is, and always will be, on the Throne. When we took communion together, I was honored to give him the bread and the cup. I placed the host in his hands.

"The body and blood of our Lord Jesus Christ, keep you in ever-lasting life."

For a brief moment, CDR Paparo and I shared in the fellowship of our God who Himself made the hard call to give up His Son so that we might have eternal life.

And in a combat zone, sometimes that is enough to heal broken hearts and strengthen us to continue on with the mission.

The two commanders at Kalagush at the dedication of the FOB chapel. PRT Commander, Commander Sam Paparo and 4-319th Commander, LTC Steve Maranian. I couldn't have asked for better men to support my religious program

Chapter Five

Cooking Steaks, Pounding Nails, and Pulling Lanyards

"We loved you so much that we were delighted to share with you not only the gospel of God but our lives as well, because you had become so dear to us." (1 Thessalonians 2:8)

The sacrifices that our Soldiers make — serving in a combat zone, away from their families and friends — can never be repaid. But I guess I am one of those people who believes freedom isn't free. The French did it for us over two hundred twenty-five years ago to give us freedom. Now we are paying it forward. Each day I was with these Soldiers, I experienced that first hand.

"It is absolutely clear that God has called us to a free life. Just make sure that you don't use this freedom as an excuse to do whatever you want to do and destroy your freedom. Rather, use your freedom to serve one another in love; that's how freedom grows." (Galatians 5:13, MSG)

When I was in Young Life, we had a saying when it came to spending time with kids. It was "earning the right to be heard." It means that we go where they are, do what they do (for the most part) and truly try to be in their world versus them coming to us. Now as a chaplain, I find that that principle really hasn't changed much. We have chaplains in the Army because we need to "be one of them." (2 Timothy 2:3) A civilian pastor really can't relate to what a Soldier goes through, not to mention what they experience on a fifteen-month deployment. If Soldiers are hungry and tired, then I am hungry and tired. If they are out in the hot sun sweating, then I am out in the hot sun sweating. In truth, I find that I earn the right to be heard every day as a chaplain.

While making my rounds on the FOB, July 4, 2007, I stopped in to our aid station. Inside, there was a young man who was holding the hand of a little girl who couldn't have been any older than two. She was being treated for an ear infection, and, even though the medics had given her some candy and a Beanie Baby animal, she seemed very scared.

What frightened me more, however, was the little bundle that the father was carrying. In his arms was a severely malnourished baby boy, not quite three months old. The local doctor who had brought this family into the clinic shared that the mother had died in childbirth and the father was too poor to provide formula for him. The docs set him up with some formula that the UN had provided every aid station near a village. They also gave him some Amoxicillin for his daughter's ear infection. As they left the clinic, I saw the local Afghan doctor tear up. "That baby will not survive the winter," he said. "It has to get better than this, doesn't it?"

It reminded me of something my pastor in Missoula once said in a sermon. He said, "If the gospel is true, then it is true for all people, everywhere, for all eternity." That means that it must be true for the Soldier who just got served divorce papers in an email attachment and is struggling wondering how that is going to affect his children. It means that it must be true for the Soldier who has to go home on emergency leave because his mother has died suddenly. It means that it must be true for the mother who is left back home to raise children on her own again while her husband is deployed — for the third time. And it means that it must be true for the Afghan father who brings his two year old daughter to our clinic to treat an ear infection while he clutches a malnourished three month old son.

"If the Son has set you free, you are free indeed." (John 8:36)

Cooking Steaks

Later on that day, I was reminded of the freedom only the Savior can give us as I stood over an open barbeque in 115 degree heat cooking steaks for the Soldiers of FOB Kalagush. Only two months into this deployment, I realized we would celebrate another Independence Day in Afghanistan before we got back home to our families. But I love being able to serve these great Soldiers. Those of us who were doing the cooking were the officers and senior Non-commissioned Officers (NCOs). These are the times, along with Thanksgiving and Christmas, where the leaders serve the Soldiers by cooking the meal and standing at the serving line as the Soldiers file by for a big steak, some ribs, and fried shrimp. No one goes away hungry!

"Hey Chaps!" the Soldiers yelled to me. "What are you cooking over there?"

"Nothing but the finest steaks for world's finest Soldiers!" I yelled back.

One Soldier looked over at me and said, "Hey, if you think about it, Chaps, you're cooking holy cow!"

The other guys standing around howled with laughter. Perhaps what was even funnier was the conversation that started because of it. During a lull in the cooking, one of the officers (a regular attendee at chapel) said, "I bet this is what it must have been like for the priests in the Old Testament times who sacrificed bulls for people's sin and all."

"Yeah," I responded. "There must have been times when the temple smelled like the Golden Corral."

The officer laughed. "But you know what? If I had been a Levitical priest during that time, I would have gotten tired of all the sacrificing that I had to do. I mean, just imagine, you just finish slaughtering and burning some cow for a guy because he was dishonest on his taxes, and then some other guy shows up and says, 'Hey Aaron, I need to sacrifice my firstborn calf because I just had sex with my secretary!' There would be a part of me that would want to strangle the guy. It would never end."

Flipping over one of the steaks, I pointed at him with my spatula and said, "Isn't it great that we don't have to do that anymore? Jesus Christ was the final sacrifice for our sins." I winked at him and smiled. "Now cooking steaks is merely for eating!"

He looked at me and said, "Thanks be to God!"

"It is for freedom that Christ has set us free." (Galatians 5:1)

Cooking steaks for the Soldiers at Kalagush on the 4ᵗʰ of July

Pounding Nails

Much of my time during the day consists of walking around the FOB chatting with Soldiers. It's actually what I love the most about this job. Still, I also spend a lot of it counseling Soldiers with problems ranging from family and domestic issues to financial and military issues. One Saturday, in particular, I will never forget.

In the mid-morning, I had a Soldier come in wanting to talk to me about his problems back home. It seems that his wife, and the mother of his three children, was having an affair with their neighbor. On the many times that this Soldier had called or written her, she professed her love to him and told him that everything was fine back home. That is, until one of the Soldiers in his unit showed him his wife's MySpace page. There, for everyone in the cyberworld to see, was a picture of her in "all of her glory." Suffice it to say, he told me it was a pose that should be reserved for his eyes only. The Soldier was devastated. She swore that it was a mistake and that she didn't want to lose him. He was struggling with what to do. His head was telling him to file for a divorce, but his heart was telling him that he still loved her, and he believed if he could just get home to see her, he could make it right. My heart ached for this Soldier. He obviously loved her very much and was heartbroken at what had happened.

This was the second counseling I had done that day involving infidelity and divorce. And the greatest challenge, when counseling is to give advice without getting emotionally involved. Unfortunately, I'm pretty sure that when it comes to marriage, I will always struggle in that arena. Call me an idealist, but I just want people to have the type of marriage that I have with my wife. It's not perfect, but it is forever, and we are willing to work out whatever differences we have; not cover them up with destructive behaviors. Needless to say, when we were finished, I was emotionally drained. Actually, I was pretty ticked off. At times, I hate the fallen world in which we live. So

I decided to go for a walk around the FOB. I headed down to the motor pool where a bunch of our mechanics were building their new vehicle bay. Nearly complete, some of them were up on the roof laying shingles. I ventured up the ladder to the roof to see how they were coming along.

"Hey fellas!" I smiled, "How's it going?"

Their team leader, Sergeant (SGT) Jason Habich, looked at me and said, "Hey chaplain! What brings you up here?" Jason was one of my faithful attendees to our Wednesday night Bible study and Sunday morning services. The few times I had spent talking with him, I learned of a man who truly loved his wife and two sons and would do anything for them. He had a marriage I wished other young non-commissioned officers had.

"Oh, just seeing if there might be a place where I could help out." I said, thinking to myself that pounding a few nails might help me relieve some frustrations.

With a surprised, somewhat dumbfounded expression, SGT Habich said, "Uh . . . sure, I guess that would be fine. Have you ever shingled a roof before?"

Now, I have to admit, there are a lot of things that our mechanics do that I would tell them I have never done. Fixed the power steering on a HUMVEE? No. Replaced the air filter in a generator? Not a chance. (I'm just glad we have guys that know how to fix them!) Hung fragmentary armor on a 5-ton? Nice try. But, as crazy as it would seem, I *have* actually shingled a roof before. Back in 1992, my wife and I, along with eight other cadets from West Point, went down to South Carolina over spring break and worked with Habitat for Humanity. The job Sue and I did? Laying shingles on the roof all week. So, when I told SGT Habich that story, he told me to grab a hammer and go to town.

Over the next couple of hours, I, along with five other Soldiers from the motor pool, shingled the whole roof. We had a great time! Several times that afternoon I had officers and senior NCOs call up to me asking what in the world I was doing.

"Hanging out, pounding nails and laying shingles!" I would happily exclaim.

One of the Soldiers who came by yelled up to me, "Hey sir, aren't you afraid you might fall?"

"Nope." I said. "After all it's just like your walk with God. If you don't think about falling, you won't fall!" (Which was exactly what the Habitat foreman had told me fifteen years before, when I WAS scared about falling!)

"Hmm . . . I guess I never thought about it like that." He said as he made his way back into the vehicle bay.

I called out after him. "Come to chapel tomorrow and I just might have some other things you may have never thought of before!"

Little did I know, that time on the roof did more than just help me to get my aggression out. It earned the right to be heard by a Soldier. The guy I issued that challenge to, showed up in chapel the very next day! Coincidence? Well, since I don't believe in coincidences, I would say it was a God-incidence. After the service, I asked him why he had decided to come.

"I liked what you said up on the roof about not falling." He said with a distinct Brooklyn accent. "Plus, any officer who will roll up his sleeves and do a little nail-pounding in the motor pool deserves to be heard at least once!"

As I took stock over the first couple of months at FOB Kalagush, I found that there had been many opportunities for me to "earn the right to be heard."

Perhaps my fondest memory of doing "ministry of presence" happened when I was on the gun line with our artillery platoon at Kalagush . . .

Pulling Lanyards

During a training exercise, doing a direct fire mission into a mountain near the FOB, one of the gun sections invited me to come and watch. I made sure I was there. To my surprise, the gun chief turned to me and said, "Chaplain, you're pulling number 5!"

"Uh . . . OK," was all I could respond with.

As the first four rounds went off, I had a number of dilemmas doing gymnastics in my head. I'm a noncombatant, does this constitute a combatant act? Well, it was a training incident and we were just firing into the side of a mountain. Am I handling the weapon if I simply pull the lanyard? Before I could answer any of these, the chief motioned me over to the Howitzer.

"Set, set, set, set!" the chief yelled.

I looked over to the gunner, SGT Pineda. Pointing at me with his hand outstretched, he yelled, "Fire!" I pulled the lanyard, and the aftershock about put me on my rear! All the redlegs were cheering like crazy. As I walked back over to the bunker, Soldiers were slapping me on the back. "Yeah, that's the way it's done, sir." And I stayed around a little longer to talk and help them clean the bore and barrel.

The next day, the chief came up to me and asked that, since they were the "hot gun" that day (the gun that needs to be ready if a fire-mission comes down), they weren't going to be able to leave the gunline to come to chapel and would it be possible for me to do a simple service for them at the bunker. I told him I would be honored to. So that Sunday, in a bunker surrounded by hundreds of HE (High Explosive) and WP (White Phosphorous) Artillery rounds, I conducted a field service for ten artillery Soldiers. We sang a couple of hymns, shared some prayer requests, and shared communion together. From then on, it became somewhat of a tradition that whichever gun was the "hot gun" I offered to come over in the afternoon and conduct a field service.

So, before you all rush to send an email to the Chief of Chaplains for fear that I may have overstepped my noncombatant boundaries as a chaplain by pulling the lanyard, I would ask for a little grace. Our Lord Jesus was often accused of eating with "tax collectors and sinners." And Paul wrote, "I have become all things to all men so that by all possible means I might save some." (1 Corinthians 9:22b). For me, the risk was worth it.

Maybe that's why the Soldiers eventually sought me out when they needed to talk about what was hurting them in life. And I'd gladly listen, and try to help them make sense of living in a fallen world telling them that it is Christ who saves them from it. Just as long as there was some type of manual labor like cooking steaks, pounding nails, or pulling lanyards that I could do afterward!

Chapter Six

Nurture the Living, Care for the Wounded, Honor the Dead

"We are therefore Christ's ambassadors, as though God were making his appeal through us. We implore you on Christ's behalf: Be reconciled to God." (2 Corinthians 5:20)

The title of this chapter is pretty much our three-fold mission in the chaplaincy — perhaps more poignantly stated while in combat. And as such, I had three major experiences early on in the deployment which put what I do every day into clear perspective for me.

Nurture the Living

"Hey, Chaplain!" A Soldier yelled to me as I walked by.

I was already in my combat gear as I was getting ready to head out with a platoon from the Provincial Reconstruction Team (PRT) on a goodwill mission to the town closest to Kalagush. The PRT has been helping to rebuild the village's girls' school there. After reading the chapter in Rashid's book, *Taliban*, entitled, "The Vanishing Gender," it did my heart good to see this school being rebuilt and many young girls getting an education.

I spun around and smiled, "Yeah, what's up, Sergeant?"

He looked at me quizzically, "You do know that you are on the bird to ABAD (short for Asadabad) in four hours right?"

"Excuse, me?" I no doubt looked surprised. "I didn't think I was supposed to fly for a couple of days yet?"

"That's true, sir." He affirmed. "But, we don't know if that flight will come or not, and so we manifested you on this flight."

Nice of them to tell me so far in advance, I thought to myself. My plan was to be gone for about two weeks visiting FOBs. I was going to take a good chunk of the day before leaving to pack, finish the field worship books that I had been working on, and make sure that my chaplain assistant had everything he needed.

"Okay." I said, smiling. "I just need an hour or so to pack."

I walked over to the guys at the vehicles and let them know a change of mission had come down for me. Even though I was disappointed, I told them that we had plenty of time to do this again. I gathered them around, said a prayer over their convoy, then headed over to tell my assistant, PFC Marshall, about our plans. I packed in about thirty minutes, and made some last minute e-mails and calls.

The bird landed right on time and we headed out to ABAD. I have to tell you though, I really wasn't prepared to go this early. My plan was to go two days later, stay two to three days, and then catch the ring route on to FOB Naray. Now it looked like I would be there for almost five days. I didn't mind being there, I just needed to get used to the mission change. Before this "hop" I had been meditating a lot on Philippians 1:22, "If I am to go on living in the body, this will mean fruitful labor for me." To me, I find that as long as the Lord gets me up in the morning, and there is still a beating heart in my chest, God still has work for me to do. I've often wanted to simply conduct my ministry through what I call "Divine Appointments." The day I got to ABAD, I got my wish.

Whenever I arrive at a FOB, I generally want to walk around and get a feel for the place. I find out where we will be sleeping, where the dining facility is, where the gym is (if they have one), and where the gunline is so I can meet up with our artillerymen. After that, I usually walk around and simply try to meet Soldiers. This is basically where my time in Young Life comes in, because it's pretty much identical to contact work. I'm thankful that contact work was my favorite thing to do in Young Life.

Marshall and I hadn't walked around for more than twenty minutes, when we spotted a squad of infantry getting ready to head back to their Vehicle Patrol Base (VPB). ABAD is the closest place to refit, so they come here to get mail, pick up supplies, etc. As I talked with the guys, I found out that two of them were from Flathead Valley, Montana. One had graduated last year from Columbia Falls, and the other had graduated two years ago from Flathead High School. I really love those small world stories!

We stood around and talked for about fifteen minutes. Once the guy driving the "gator" (a John Deere four-wheeler) came with all their mail, it was time for them to mount up. I asked the squad leader if I could pray for their convoy. The sergeant said, "Roger that, sir," then at the top of his voice said, "Hey! Get you're a**es over here, the chaplain wants to say an f*#%$ng prayer!" I can safely say that I've never heard a call for worship quite like that before, but the guys came right over and gathered in a circle ready for the chaplain.

I told them about God's protection and Joshua 1:9. I assured them of the great work they were doing and encouraged them to persevere with 2 Chronicles 15:7, "Be strong and do not give up, for your work will be rewarded." Then I said a prayer over this mighty group of Paratroopers, and they got into their vehicles. As I turned, I called out to them to stay encouraged.

Just then, the squad leader called out to me. "Hey sir, you got a minute?"

"Sure, sergeant, what's up?" I asked, removing my sunglasses. This was a guy who truly looked the part of an infantry squad leader. Only five foot, eight inches but built like a solid brick wall, his eyes were a steel grey, and he had a square chin. His patrol cap sat high on his high-and-tight shaved head. I was sure that if he took off his ACU blouse there would be at least one tattoo on his arm with something like "Kill 'em all, and let God sort 'em out!" But once he came closer, I could see that there was something truly bothering him.

"I, uh . . ." he stammered. "I didn't want to say anything around my guys because I didn't want them to worry." I nodded, knowing that he must feel like he needs to always be strong for his guys.

"You see, I was wondering if you would remember to pray for my family. I found out yesterday that my mother, sister and brother were all involved in a rollover car accident." He was starting to get choked up as tears filled his eyes. "A drunk driver came over into their lane and hit them head on causing the car to go off the road. My brother is in critical condition and they don't know if he's going to make it."

I gently put my arm around his shoulders and said, "Sergeant, you're at the top of my prayer list. But would you mind if we prayed right now?" He quietly agreed and we bowed our heads to pray. When we said, "Amen," he said to me, "Thanks, Chaplain. I've never had someone pray over my squad before. So when you did that, I knew you were the guy I wanted to talk to about my family. I really believe God is with you, sir."

"Sergeant, God is with you, too. I believe He is here to protect your boys and keep you safe. Seek Him out my friend, and you'll find Him — I promise." With that, he walked over to his vehicle and they headed out the gate.

If just for that one guy, I would have known that God's plan and divine appointments were perfect. I understood at that moment why He wanted me at ABAD two days early. Or so I thought I did. But that evening, I would be reminded once again.

Care for the Wounded

I stood as close to the back wall as I could of the Tactical Operations Center (TOC) at ABAD looking at the double plasma screen at the front of the room which had a map of the operational battlespace. As evening had fallen into darkest night (illumination was close to zero) several patrols had come under fire and were currently considered "Troops in Contact" (TIC). I watched the screen and listened to the Radio Telephone Operator (RTO). It had begun to rain where one of the platoons were under fire, and the report came back that they had taken casualties. One Killed in Action (KIA) and one Wounded in Action (WIA). Medical Evacuation (MEDEVAC) had been requested, and they were headed to the Field Surgical Team (FST) site at ABAD. As soon as I heard the choppers touch down, I headed down to the FST.

The Soldier on the table had suffered a gunshot wound to the chest. It was right underneath his shoulder and, thank God, was not life-threatening, but they still had to work fast to prevent blood from pooling around his lungs. As I walked over to the doctor's table, there was a flurry of activity. One nurse was setting up an IV, the other was taking his pulse. The surgeon was asking him questions — his name, what hurt, etc. The OR tech was moving the portable X-ray machine into place over his chest while yet another squirted "jelly" onto his abdomen to take an ultrasound.

My first thought was, "How can I get over to this Soldier without seeming like I'm in the way?" One nurse yelled to me to grab the cart next to me that held the ultrasound machine. I said, "No problem," and wheeled it over to him. With such a flurry of activity, it reminded me of all the *ER* episodes I had seen — especially when I looked down at the Soldier. His first name was Frank, and he looked pretty scared. With every move that a doctor or nurse made, his eyes darted over in that direction. He knew that he needed their care, but having just been in a firefight, I imagined that his adrenaline was still running pretty high, and so were his nerves.

I made my way around the docs and over to his hand. I took it in mine and squeezed it. He moved his head to look over at me. His mouth covered by an oxygen mask, he didn't say much, but his eyes seemed to immediately get soft. Here was someone who was just here to give him comfort without sticking him or prodding him.

"Hey, Frank," I said reaching over with my other hand to stroke his head. "You're doing great buddy. These guys are the best surgical team in Afghanistan and they're gonna take good care of you, OK?"

He nodded.

I continued to hold his hand and ask where he was from. When he told me he was from the Virginia Beach area, I asked him if he had ever been to Busch Gardens Williamsburg. He said he had many times, and I reminded him that they still give free admission to veterans of OIF and OEF. (He laughed when I told him that I saved a bunch of money taking my family of six there after OIF II!) Before we knew it, they had stabilized him and were ready to bring him back up to the MEDEVAC helicopter.

As they bundled him up, I got down and put my mouth close to his ear. I whispered to him Joshua 1:9 and told him to stay strong and courageous. He nodded and closed his eyes. I wanted to give him something to hang on to. Then I remembered the Shield of Strength that I had on my dogtag chain. I quickly took it off and slipped it into the palm of his hand.

He looked at it and then looked at me. "Thanks, sir." He whispered. They got him back on the ambulance and headed up to the landing zone (LZ).

After the ambulance left, I asked if I might be able to go up to the LZ and pray over the KIA Soldier. They told me I wouldn't make it up there before they took off. So as I walked back to my hooch, I prayed as the helicopter lifted off the LZ and flew overhead. The next day I read about the KIA and knew it was going to hit our brigade hard.

Honor the Dead

The article in the Stars and Stripes newspaper read, "19-year-old private, son of 173rd's senior-enlisted Soldier, is killed in Afghanistan" CSM Vimoto, the Brigade Command Sergeant Major, learned only hours after the MEDEVAC lifted off from ABAD, that it was his son, PFC Timothy Vimoto, who had been killed during an ambush near Asadabad.

As is customary, a Soldier will always escort the fallen Soldier back to his duty station and then on to their home for burial. The ramp ceremony in the military is one of the most solemn and honoring things we do for our fallen heroes. It grips all who participate in it. But I'm sure that this one gripped its participants even more. A highly decorated combat Paratrooper had to do what few ever want to do — bury the son who had followed in his footsteps.

I wasn't there when CSM Vimoto heard the news, but my fellow chaplain, CH (CPT) Mike Hart, was stationed in Jalalabad with the Brigade Headquarters. When I arrived there a couple days later, he told me about it. "He just wept on my shoulder in his office, and I just let him cry," Mike said. A great brother in the Lord and a veteran chaplain, I was glad Mike was there to care for a "wounded" father and help him to honor his loss.

Still at War

During the deployment, I was amazed at how often the war in Afghanistan had become the "forgotten war." Most of the money was being spent in Iraq, most of the equipment and troops were over there as well.[1] But the threat was just as real in Afghanistan as in Iraq. In fact, by the summer of 2007, Soldiers in Afghanistan had an equal if not greater chance of becoming a casualty as they did in Iraq. No, this war, although not reported much in the media, is still a viable fight, and one that we must win.

Again, the reality of that statement became all too true for me when I was asked to participate in a ramp ceremony a month later for one of our fallen Soldiers. During a ramp ceremony, pall bearers place the remains of fallen warriors onto an aircraft that will transport them home. The Soldier, a platoon sergeant with the 2nd Battalion, 503rd Infantry, was killed in a fire fight on the day that all the chaplains arrived at Bagram Air Field. Naturally, the chaplain assigned to that unit, CH Schnarr, made the necessary preparations to receive the Soldier at the airfield and then send him on to the states. I was asked by the 82nd Airborne Division Chaplain, CH (LTC) Laigaie, to choose a reading for the ceremony.

It is hard to put into words all the emotions and feelings one has during a ramp ceremony. Everything on Bagram Air Field comes to a stop, if only briefly, in order for those who are stationed there to come to the road and salute while the flag-draped coffin is transported to the plane. Soldiers in formation line the runway to the plane, standing at attention in somber

---

[1] In October 2009, President Barack Obama approved sending 13,000 additional troops to Afghanistan, primarily in the role of support (engineers, medical specialists, intelligence experts and military police). This brought the authorized build-up to 34,000 troops – twice what was in Afghanistan when the 173rd Brigade was there. Most of this buildup was the result of huge drawdown in Iraq culminating in a total force remaining of only 50,000 by December 2010.

silence. When the coffin arrives, the color guard moves forward towards the plane with the chaplains in step right behind. A slow hymn is played by the band (that day it was "Holy, Holy, Holy") as we lead the pall bearers to the front of the aircraft.

I stood there at attention while the casket was readied for transport. The pall bearers placed the coffin on the bed of the plane, stepped back and saluted. Then in almost perfect precision, they all knelt down on one knee, placing one hand on the coffin, bowed their heads and prayed. As they left the aircraft, my friend and fellow chaplain, CH Hart read his Scripture. Next, it was my turn. Almost overcome by emotion with tears streaming down my face, I read from Psalm 27:1-4:

> *The LORD is my light and my salvation; whom shall I fear? The LORD is the stronghold of my life; of whom shall I be afraid? When evildoers assail me to eat up my flesh, my adversaries and foes, it is they who stumble and fall. Though an army encamps against me, my heart shall not fear; though wars arise against me, yet I will be confident. One thing have I asked of the LORD, that will I seek after: that I may dwell in the house of the LORD all the days of my life.*

We stood as the division chaplain called out a final prayer, and watched as each Soldier came up the ramp to pay their final respects to this fallen warrior. Finally, the four of us walked over to the casket, knelt down on one knee, and prayed as well.

As we came down the stairs on the front of the aircraft, the Brigade Commander and Brigade Command Sergeant Major were there to shake our hands. It had been a difficult first four months for our brigade. That death marked the twelfth fallen Soldier. I looked into the eyes of my Brigade Commander, Colonel Charles Preysler. He looked tired. When he extended out his hand, I took it, then drew him in to hug him. "You're doing a great job, sir," I said so only he could hear. "And I am honored to have you as my commander."

He smiled and thanked me for my continued prayers and ministry to his Soldiers. As I walked away, I prayed that he would find the time to grieve as well. I realized that both his job and my job just may be the two loneliest jobs in theater. No one really thinks to check on how the brigade commander is doing. Most look to him for guidance and command decisions, all the while forgetting that this is a man with a wife and family back home as well. He grieves the loss of his Soldiers more than any other because he is the one who authorizes the operations, knowing full well that some in his charge will not be going home to their wives and children. And he is the one who personally writes letters of condolences to every family who loses a son or daughter. By the time the 173rd would head home, he would have written more than forty letters home. How hard it must be!

And so as a chaplain, I weep when others can't. I pray when others don't know how. And I offer words of encouragement and strength when there seem to be no words left to say. I must admit, however, it is often a lonely place to be. Yet it is what the Lord has called me to do in support of those who would fight and die for our country.

All this reminded me of my training back at Chaplain School earlier in the year. During our Capstone Exercise (CPX), I struggled to know what to do during a Mass Casualty (MasCal) exercise and wanted to get over the feeling of not knowing what to do and feeling like I was in the way. One of the instructors and a great mentor to many of us new chaplains, CH (LTC) Jason Duckworth, put his hand on my shoulder and said, "Don't worry, Don. When it happens, your training will kick in and you'll know what to do." His words rang true for me on the battlefields of Afghanistan.

Nurture the living, care for the wounded, honor the dead. This is what we are called to do every day out here. We can't do one and not the others. Some of us may be more comfortable with nurturing the living. Others may be better with trauma and knowing what to do to care for the wounded. And all of us, I imagine, struggle with honoring the dead. But like a stool that has three legs, all of them need to be done with care and love.

Someday, Lord willing, this war will be over and we will never again have to send heroes home in flag draped coffins to their loved ones. But until that day, I cling to the end of Psalm 27:

> *I am still confident of this — that I shall look upon the goodness of the LORD in the land of the living! Wait for the LORD; be strong, and let your heart take courage; wait for the LORD! (Psalm 27:13-14)*

I'm honored to be called chaplain — called to bring truth to the living Soldiers, hope to the wounded ones, and reverence for those whom have given all for the cause of freedom.

Chapter Seven

OPs, IEDs and Fire Missions

"Consider it pure joy, my brothers, whenever you face trials of many kinds, because you know that the testing of your faith develops perseverance. Perseverance must finish its work so that you may be mature and complete, not lacking anything."
(James 1:2-4)

Not long into the deployment, many of the Soldiers nick-named me the "Circuit Riding Preacher" because of all the traveling I did. Throughout the year, our battalion had Soldiers at as many as thirteen different FOBs in the north-eastern part of Afghanistan, so it was necessary for me to travel quite a bit. I made it a goal to visit each FOB at least twice before my mid-tour leave.

Most of the FOBs were austere and remote. Yet none compared to our firing platoon who called FOB Lybert home. I remember looking out the window of the Chinook helicopter on our approach to the FOB. This patrol base was something right out of the Vietnam era. It reminded me of every Vietnam war movie I had ever seen. Built right on the side of a moun-tain, you get your physical training just walking up and down from your hooch! About one hundred eighty families live in the village down below. No running water, no electricity. It's something right out of the middle ages. Even so, the view was absolutely spectacular. It was like looking at Shangri La. At sunset, it took your breath away. On one of my visits, one Soldier told me that he looked forward to the evening every single day. I had to agree with him. Looking down from the FOB into the valley gave you a glimpse of God's magnificent creation, even in a combat zone.

Yet the strategic significance of Lybert could be overlooked. Situated not more than a few kilometers from the Pakistan border, the valley it overwatches was known as a "rat trail" for the Taliban to come from Pakistan. In reading the book, *Taliban*, you learn that most of the fighters come from schools known as madrasas. These schools teach the fundamental teachings of the Koran, and convince their students that bringing a pure Islamic state to the world is a just cause. On several occasions, the Taliban leaders have called on more fighters, and the "deans" of the madrasas have literally shut down their schools to send young men off to fight in Afghanistan. So, when it comes to men who would fight alongside the Taliban, I guess you could say that conscription into their army is alive and well.

OPs

While we were at Lybert, I expressed a desire to hike up the mountain to the observation post (OP) to see the Soldiers who spend the better part of a week or two up there. So, early one morning, the first sergeant, the sergeant major, my assistant, PFC Marshall, and I, began our trek up the mountain. And I can safely tell you that this mountain was no small hill. To put it bluntly, it made hiking to the "M" in Missoula, Montana, look like a kiddie ride at the state fair! The first leg of the climb was about a seventy degree incline. There were times when you were literally crawling on your hands and knees (pretty vertical mind you) in order to get up to the plateau. And we did that about three times in the climb. At one point, it looked like we weren't going to make it because my chaplain assistant, PFC Marshall, was really struggling. I had been starting to get a little concerned about how much Physical Training (PT) he was doing, so we started to run around the FOB three times a week. Marshall doesn't like to run, but he knows it is necessary if we are both to survive in combat.

"I don't think I can make it, sir." Marshall said, taking a knee on the route.

"I know it's hard, my friend," I said smiling. "But take a look at how far you've already come! We're over halfway there. Trust me, it's all going to be worth it once we reach the top!"

Marshall didn't look too convinced. So I got down on one knee with him and put my arm around his shoulder. "OK, let's try and tackle this one step at a time. And each time we finish a leg of the climb, if you want to quit, then we can stop and go back down," I said, trying to be as motivating as possible to the man who carries a weapon so I don't have to.

"OK, sir. But only to the next leg." He said standing up and taking a drink from his CamelBak.

And that's the way it went for the next hour. I would point out a tree not twenty-five meters away and we would climb to that one and take a break. But before he could say he was ready to quit, I showed him the next tree. "That one doesn't look that far," he would say. "Let's get to that one. I'll probably want to quit after that." Before he knew it, we were fifty meters from the gate of the OP, and the handful of Soldiers that were there were cheering him on and encouraging him to keep going! You would have thought we had just reached the summit of Everest! And for Marshall, I guess we had. For when we got to the top, and saw the beauty that was all around, it took your breath away!

"Hey Chaps!" One of the guards yelled with a smile from ear to ear. "Welcome to our humble OP! The living may not be the Ritz, but the view is amazing!" I couldn't have agreed more.

The normal rotation for these guys was they come up for a week or two to the OP (which is just on the other side of a mountain separating Afghanistan and Pakistan) and simply watch the "rat trail." But the guys seemed to really enjoy it. They didn't have any running water or electricity, so they cooked their meals over an open flame, and took showers by putting liter bottles of water out in the sun.

As we sat around the fire eating our breakfast, Soldiers told me of the many things they have seen being up there. There were the typical shepherds tending to the villages' goats. There was the farmer who climbs up to offer them homemade bread (more like unleavened pita bread). Perhaps the most bizarre story was when a gypsy woman came from over the mountain with her ten-year old daughter wanting to sell her to the Soldiers for fifty dollars. To us, the very thought of selling your child to Soldiers is deplorable. To the gypsy, it was simply a way to help feed her eleven other children on the other side of the mountain. Fifty dollars is over a month's wages for Afghans. Rather than buy the child, however, the Soldiers did offer to let her work on the OP—picking up trash, gathering water, etc. That way, the woman would be paid on a weekly basis and she wouldn't be selling her daughter into slavery. Sadly, though, the gypsy turned down the offer.

"I got the feeling from talking to her," said the sergeant-in-charge of the OP. "That she didn't want her to work, she just wanted to get rid of her." Tears began to fill his eyes. "How could someone do that to their own kid?" And for once, I didn't have an answer. But all the way back down the mountain, I prayed for our Soldiers, that gypsy woman, and someone to give her hope beyond her present circumstances.

That evening, we had a small worship service. Only a handful of Soldiers came, but the backdrop of the sun setting over the valley reminded us of the Creator God whom we worship.

SPC Marshal and me at FOB Lybert after our return from the OP above the camp.

IEDs

Thankfully, the resupply helicopter that dropped us off at Lybert came back around to pick us up a few days later. After an overnight stay at FOB Naray and getting some much needed rest and fellowship with my friend and fellow chaplain, Chaplain Kelly O'Lear, we headed over to Asadabad (ABAD) to check in with our guns there. The day we arrived, I went over to the Tactical Operations Cell (TOC) to check us in. All was well, and we easily found an open bed to sleep in for the night.

As I walked out of the TOC, a navy chief stopped me and asked, "Are you the chaplain for this FOB?" I told him that I wasn't, but since there was no chaplain assigned, those of us who have Soldiers in ABAD try to cover it whenever we can.

"Well, in that case, you might want to walk over and talk to those guys right over there," he said pointing to a squad of

Soldiers standing around their Humvees. "They just came back from quite a fight, and an IED exploded right in front of one of their vehicles. Amazingly, not one of them was injured or killed."

Taking his lead, I walked over to those Soldiers. I didn't recognize any of them, so they weren't any of my guys. "Hey guys, how are you doing?" (Easily the dumbest question I have ever asked.)

"Well, sir," said the squad leader. "How the h*%$ do you think we are? We just came from almost getting our heads blown off from an f#@$ing IED and then were engaged by the enemy at pretty close range. I would say that my squad has been through a lot today, and it isn't even noon!"

"I would definitely have to agree with you there," I said. "But, hey, what a miracle that you all came back here alive, right?"

"Yeah," he shrugged. "I guess so."

"You guess so?" I repeated. "Son, take a look around you. All of your Soldiers are not only intact, they don't even have a scratch on them. And from what you have been through, I would say that that is nothing short of a miracle. God supernaturally protected you!"

"Yeah?" He glared at me through his protective glasses. "Well, I don't know how many more miracles like this I can take. Look chaplain, thanks for the talk, and for coming to encourage my guys. It means a lot to them. But I'm not the type that believes in God. We made it through that simply by chance." And with that, he walked away toward the dining facility.

As I watched him walk away, my mind flashed back to the many times at the high school where I, as a Young Life leader, would try to get kids to look beyond the present into things eternal. Did those times make a difference? Do they make a difference now when so much is at stake? I don't know. I talked with a few more of the Soldiers in the squad, and then I made my way to the chow hall.

Fire Missions

The young section chief sat across from me shaking his head. Hearing that I was at ABAD, he made an appointment through his Smoke (the platoon sergeant) to talk with me.

"You know sir," he said leaning forward in his chair to rest his forearms on his legs. "This deployment is a lot different than the others for me."

"Oh yeah," I said leaning in as well. "Tell me what makes it different."

"Well, for my last deployment, we were in Iraq," he explained. "And we were pretty much a maneuver element. We didn't have a firing mission. But for some reason, I think that I felt more in control then than I do now."

"How so?" I asked.

"I mean, last deployment, when we would go out of the wire," he explained. "I felt like we were taking the fight to the enemy, and I had some sense of control. But now, we are simply waiting for fire missions to come down, and our greatest threat comes from the possibility of a rocket or mortar hitting this FOB. But I don't know if or when that is going to happen, and I don't like the feeling of not being in control."

The two of us sat in silence for a little while as I tried to grapple with what this Soldier was saying. There was a part of me that understood that by "taking the fight to the enemy" it felt more like it was on your terms rather than on theirs. All through our military training we are taught that the best defense is a good offense and you only stay in a defense long enough to rest and refit before heading back out on offense again. So, I kind of understood why he would be feeling this way. But deep down, it was simply the question of control.

"Sergeant, can I ask you — do you have a faith?" I asked matter-of-factly.

"Uhh . . ." he shifted in his seat. "Not really. I mean my wife is the one who has the religion in our family. She's the one who makes sure that our kids go to church and all. I mean, I grew up going to church, but I figure I really don't need that now."

I smiled and replied, "Well, what if I told you that you're never in control in either of those situations? What if I told you that you going out of the wire on a patrol in Iraq or you staying inside the FOB awaiting a fire mission are the same when it comes to God? You have no more control on patrol than you do inside the gun bunker."

He looked at me and nodded his head in understanding. "I guess I know what you mean. It would make sense in some ways. You see, on one of the patrols in Iraq, one of my Soldiers was killed right in front of me when the vehicle he was in ran over an IED." The sergeant began to choke up. "And I remember feeling like that could have been me and my truck instead of his." He was crying in earnest now. "But sir, he was just a young kid. He was only twenty and left behind a wife and two small children. How could God allow that to happen?"

I took a deep breath and replied, "Sergeant, I don't know all the answers of why God allows this person to die and not that person. What I *do* know is that God is sovereign, and He is good. And all these things that we go through in this fallen world are meant to bring us to Him. You're right, you could have been the one who was killed in that IED attack two years ago, but you weren't. And I think it is because God wanted to get you to this point right here, right now."

We sat and talked for the next hour or so. He asked a lot of questions, and I did my best to answer him. In the end, however, there was really only one question to ask.

Opening my pocket New Testament, I looked this young Soldier straight in the eye and said, "Sergeant, the Bible says, 'in the time of my favor I heard you, and in the day of salvation I helped you. I tell you now is the time of God's favor, now is the day of salvation.' (2 Corinthians 6:2). I believe that God has brought you to this place in time so you can make a decision for eternity. Don't you want to know that whether you are on fire missions on the FOB or out on patrol, your soul can be at peace?"

Through tears he looked at me and said, "Yes sir, I think I do."

So right then, this young sergeant and I grabbed hands and we prayed. It wasn't a fancy prayer, or one to write down for keeps later. But it was genuine. The wrestling with God for this Soldier was over—he had given his life to Christ!

That evening, I held a field service on the gun line in the "ready" bunker. Many of the Soldiers from the firing platoon came, including that young sergeant. We had just finished singing a couple of praise songs when over the bunker radio screamed the command, "Fire Mission, Fire Mission, Fire Mission!"

Half the platoon raced out of the bunker to their gun. To be honest, I really didn't know what to do at that point. Here I was, in the middle of a field service at a ready bunker, and a fire mission has come down. Do I keep going? Do I tell the Soldiers we'll continue when the mission is over with?

"Well," I said smiling. "Uh, maybe we should grab hands and pray." So we did.

"Lord Jesus," I prayed. "We lift up the Soldiers that are right now in a fire fight outside this FOB. We pray that You would protect them. Send Your angels to cover their movement. Get them out of the kill zone. We also thank You that as the artillery, when our fellow Soldiers call for fire, we can send support to them. Thank You for the awesome fire power that we have."

No sooner had I said "fire power" did we hear "Boom!" The door to the bunker flew open and my makeshift altar with the communion elements shook like crazy. The sound was deafening. Those of us who were still inside the bunker looked at each other. And the Soldier who, just hours before, had accepted Christ into his life, smiled and yelled, "Amen!"

There really wasn't much else to say.

That field service will go down in my journal as one of the most memorable. Not because of the attendance or because of the songs we sang, but because it was where the sacred touched the secular — where we as Soldiers, called to do a mission, stopped long enough to remember that God authored all of it as part of his sovereign plan.

> *"No, in all things we are more than conquerors through him who loved us. For I am convinced that neither death nor life, neither angels nor demons, neither the present nor the future, nor any powers, neither height nor depth, nor anything else in all creation, will be able to separate us from the love of God that is in Christ Jesus our Lord." (Romans 8:37-38)*

And for that I say, *Amen*.

Chapter Eight

From Calm, to Chaos, to Comfort

"Even though I walk through the valley of the shadow of death, I will fear no evil, for you are with me; your rod and your staff, they comfort me." (Psalm 23:4)

On July 23, 2007, Major Tom Bostick was killed when his vehicle was struck by an IED. To be honest, Major Bostick was just another name to me until I found out that my good friends, Ryan Burke, our S-2 (intelligence officer), and Tom Donatelle, our Headquarters and Headquarters Battery (HHB) Commander, were pretty close to him. Ryan had served with him in the Ranger Regiment, and Tom served with him a couple of years ago back here in Afghanistan. Major Bostick was leading a convoy back to FOB Keating after meeting with local elders near Kamu Village when it was ambushed by insurgents. He and one of his company's squad leaders, SSG William R. Fritsche, were killed during the ensuing fire fight, and another thirteen American Soldiers were wounded in the engagement. When the news hit, I knew that I needed to find my friends, Tom and Ryan.

I found Tom sitting where we at FOB Kalagush have come to call "The Settin' Place." After dinner, a few of us would usually go to this little porch built on the side of one of the

B-Huts complete with deck chairs and a place for Soldiers to discard their cigarette butts. Staring into space with a cigarette in his hand, I could tell he was grieving the loss of his friend.

"Hey, Tom," I said, "I'm sorry to hear about your loss."

He looked up at me through his sunglasses. "Yeah, it really sucks," he said, his voice a little shaky. "This one hits a little close to home, you know?"

"I know, brother," I replied, sitting down in the chair next to him. "Is there anything I can do?"

He shrugged his shoulders. "No, I don't think so. I mean, I guess when it's your time to go, it's your time to go."

I nodded. I wanted to say something. I wanted to have a verse come to my mind that would bring him comfort, but the ones that did seemed, well to be quite candid, trite. It's not that the Word of God is trite, but the verses that kept on coming to mind just didn't seem to fit. Should I pull out my pocket New Testament and read from 1 Corinthians 15? Or maybe I could tell him about the coming of the Lord as Paul so wonderfully describes it in 1 Thessalonians 4? I could have done that, but somehow, the time just didn't seem right. So we just sat there — Tom looking off into the horizon, and me staring at the ground. We probably stayed that way for ten or fifteen minutes.

Eventually, Tom broke the silence. He sighed and said, "Thanks for being here, Don."

And that's when it hit me. Simply being there was better than any verse or platitude I could come up with. It reminded me of what Job's friends did for him when he had just experienced traumatic loss.

"Job's friends set out from their homes and met together by agreement to go and sympathize with him and comfort him. When they saw him from a distance, they could hardly recognize him, they began to weep aloud, and the tore their robes and sprinkled dust on their heads. Then they sat on the ground with him for

*seven days and seven nights. No one said a word to him, because
they saw how great his suffering was." (Job 2:11b-13, emphasis
mine)*

I didn't need to say anything. I just needed to be there.
Saint Francis of Assisi was right when he said, "Preach the
gospel always, and when necessary, use words."

Over the next few weeks, I would watch my friend Tom
go from being a battery commander in name and position, to
being a leader whose Soldiers would follow him anywhere in
battle. In the events that were to come, he would lead them
through chaos and bring them comfort.

The Calm

Later that week, I was scheduled to start moving about the
battlefield to visit our Soldiers. As crazy as it is to get from one
place to another in this country, there were still two FOBs at
which our Soldiers were located that I had yet to visit. It was
the intent of my commander that before I started to revisit
FOBs, I would at least get to each location once. So it was
with this trip. While I was planning on getting to Lybert again
to help out a fellow chaplain in the area, I was also planning
to get to Khogyani and Blessing. And as Proverb 16:9 says, I
had planned out my course, but because air assets sometimes
come at a premium out here, it truly is the Lord who directed
our steps!

"All who are scheduled to go to Khogyani, the flight is
cancelled," the Navy Chief called out to us.

It was now the middle of the night at Kalagush. The flight
had been on again, off again now for the better part of twelve
hours. So, when the chief let us know that it really was cancelled, I simply picked up my gear and headed back to my
hooch.

My last conscious thought before I fell asleep was, "Well,
Lord, you must have a reason for me to stay here, so here I

am." And like I had done so often, I thought of Philippians 1:22, "If I am to go on living in the body, it will mean fruitful labor for me." I only wish I knew what kind of fruitful labor it was going to be. However, by lunchtime the next day, I was sure to find out.

The Chaos

As I sat down to eat lunch, I hadn't taken more than three bites when I noticed that something wasn't right. What normally was a calm dining facility with people enjoying their lunch watching whatever American Forces Network (AFN) was showing on the TV at the time, turned into a tense, chaotic meal. Tom, who was sitting next to me and the First Sergeant, was given a situation report in his ear by one of his Soldiers and he raced out of the room. Before I knew it, several Soldiers around me, all part of our security detail jumped up and headed out the door as well.

One of the civilians who faithfully attend chapel each week, Mason Geer, was walking by so I grabbed him by the arm and asked what was going on.

"I don't know for sure, sir," he said with a fearful look on his face. "But all I know is that one of our patrols has come under contact on their way back to the FOB and there's word one Soldier's been killed."

Leaving my tray on the table, I raced out the door to the aid station. The docs there had already laid out four litters, and the medics were briefing the litter bearers on what actions to take once the wounded arrived. When I could see that one of the docs could break free, I asked him what he knew.

Initial reports coming in were that one of our patrols had been ambushed on its way back to the FOB. It was believed that one of the vehicles had hit an IED. From what he could discern from the radio chatter, there were three WIA, one KIA, and one uninjured, and the patrol was making its way back to the FOB with the wounded.

Out of the corner of my eye, I could see that Captain Donatelle (Tom) had mustered his men together and was about to launch them as the QRF. Time was of the essence, so I ran over to the vehicles just as their platoon leader was giving them a quick operations brief. The intel officer was there and he had quickly printed out maps of the ambush site for each TC (truck commander). I could tell that these Soldiers were tense. This was the real thing. They didn't know what they would face once they rolled outside the wire, but they were ready. It was go time.

Just then, one of the artillery guns from the gunline sounded off with a thunderous "Boom!" Our Soldiers in the ambush had called for fire. Having gotten to know the guys pretty well from the field services I gave each Sunday, I knew that their fires would be accurate. "At least that will keep the enemy's head down," I thought.

I walked down the line to each vehicle. "This is what you have been trained for, guys!" I yelled. "Now is the time to be strong and courageous! Your fellow Soldiers need you." I put my arm around each TC and told them I would be praying. As the vehicles rolled out of the gate, I held up my fist then brought it to my chest signaling to each Soldier, "Strength and Honor."

Not more than five minutes passed when we heard the MEDEVAC birds flying in. Originally, we had thought the plan was to bring the wounded back to the FOB and then send them off, but in the chaos of the fight, the decision was made to launch the helicopters to an LZ close to where the action was. So with an Apache escort and an A-10 Warthog flying overhead for closer air support, the MEDEVAC bird flew in and, within minutes, the wounded were flown out of there on their way to the nearest FST Aid Station.

Now we just needed to wait for the patrol to return. For me, it seemed like an eternity. Many of our Soldiers were still standing around waiting to assist our brothers in arms. I walked over to a group standing near the aid station to ask if they wanted to pray. They all nodded, and we grabbed hands to pray for the Soldiers who had been wounded, and for those yet to return. No sooner did we say "Amen," then the patrol vehicles started coming in the gate. The medics and I ran up to the vehicles. The Soldiers got out of the vehicles, throwing off their protective vests. I could tell that they were exhausted. I moved over to one Soldier and caught him just before he collapsed. He was drenched with sweat and was crying. I put his arm over my shoulder and walked him to the aid station. Thankfully, other than heat exhaustion and some ringing ears from the blast, the rest of the squad was fine. Once they had been checked out, they were released to get cleaned up.

While the medics checked each of them out, they began to relay what had happened. The Soldier, SGT Lee, was uninjured in the vehicle that endured the blast. He shared that they were driving along when suddenly he heard a huge blast. Five seconds later, there was another. When he turned to grab his weapon, he saw that his gunner, SGT Taureen Harris, was down. SGT Lee tried to drive the vehicle out of the kill zone but he couldn't steer the wheel. The vehicle came to a stop after hitting a wall. The other vehicles in the convoy provided cover as the wounded and driver were taken out of the vehicle. But the gunner, who was already dead, was enmeshed in wires and debris, and they couldn't get him out. That's when the fire started. The squad leader pushed everyone away from the vehicle as fire from the blast residue caught the ammunition inside. Within minutes, the entire vehicle was engulfed in flames.

It would be impossible to put into words all the feelings and emotions that were experienced that day. There would be the Soldiers on the QRF who provided security on the vehicle that felt helpless to do anything for their brother trapped in the vehicle. Not knowing if he was alive or dead, many shared that they thought if they could have gotten him out, he might have survived. (Later reports would show that the ambush was initiated by an RPG launched from the hills above the patrol. It went right through the gunner's hatch. SGT Harris was dead before he hit the floor of the vehicle.)

There would be the Soldiers out on the initial patrol who felt guilty because the patrol had taken longer than expected. If they had returned an hour earlier, maybe the attack wouldn't have happened. Then there were the docs who had to hold it together emotionally while they identified the remains. Or even me; who, as the chaplain, tries to ensure that I pray with every patrol that rolls outside the gates of Kalagush. I never even knew there was a patrol scheduled that day. If I had prayed over the patrol, would the outcome have still been the same? My belief in a Sovereign God says, "Yes," but my heart wishes it were different.

At one point, the Soldiers of Headquarter Battery, acting as the QRF, were told that they would have to go out again that night to secure the area after the remains had been brought back to the FOB. Murmurings of anger, frustration, and fear rumbled through the ranks. After an update brief at the TOC, I told Tom about some of the Soldiers' frustrations. He wasted no time. He had the first sergeant gather the maneuver platoon by their vehicles. He asked me to be there to offer a prayer after he spoke. What he said will stay with me for the rest of my life.

Tom and I arrived at the vehicles just after the platoon leader had given his brief. He gave Tom the final word. With a steel-eyed look and a Patton stance, CPT Donatelle addressed his men.

"I've heard that there are some of you who are angry that we have to go back out there tonight," he said, moving his gaze to look at each of his Soldiers. "And there may be some of you who are wondering why you all, our headquarters battery made up of mechanics, weather and NBC Soldiers, are being asked to do this mission."

Tom paused, then said in a strong command voice, "Because the bottom line is, we are all combat Soldiers first! Guys, one of our men is still out there. Now I know he's dead, but we never leave a buddy behind in this brigade. So we are going to go out there and bring him back. We are going to provide security for our medics recovering his remains. And we are going to close with and destroy the enemy if we have to do it."

All the Soldiers had their eyes locked on their battery commander. There was no doubt in their minds who was in charge as he finished. "If there are any of you who weren't sure if this was the real deal or not, guess what? It's the real deal, and you all need to have your heads one hundred percent in it. Now the chaplain's going to offer up a prayer for our mission, and then we will mount up to do what we came here to do."

As I got ready to pray, I couldn't help but see that my friend had truly become a commander that night. CPT Donatelle's men came to trust him in a way that few commanders ever get from their men. They would follow him to the very gates of hell after that — even if they knew they would not come back. My prayer was that they would have courage for the mission, but I knew they already had it. Tom had brought calm in the midst of chaos.

Perhaps the hardest thing I had to do that night was say a prayer over the remains of the Soldier. By the time our guys had recovered the remains, it was late in the evening. Our two Physician Assistants, Doc Sandifer and Doc Ashby, brought the body bag into the maintenance shed. I had asked that before they opened it, if we, along with the Soldiers who had brought him in, could gather around the remains and pray. They all grabbed hands and formed a circle around the body. I knelt down and placed my hands on the body bag. It was still warm from the fire. I prayed a prayer from the Armed Forces Prayer Book:

"O God, who by the glorious resurrection of your Son Jesus Christ destroyed death, and brought life and immortality to light: Grant that your

servant, SPC Harris, being raised with Him, may know the strength of His presence, and rejoice in His eternal glory; who with you and the Holy Spirit lives and reigns, one God, forever and ever. Amen"

The Comfort

Over the next few days, I would come to learn much of SGT Taurean T. Harris. A massive man, he was a Soldier's Soldier. Originally, trained as a heating and air conditioning mechanic, he was assigned to the 202nd Military Intelligence Battalion as a gunner for one of the intelligence collection teams. He made friends very quickly, and it didn't matter if you were a part of the 4-319th or a part of the Provincial Reconstruction Team, he treated everyone the same. He had a great smile and a gentle demeanor about him. He didn't talk a lot, but when he did, he always had an encouraging word to say. The father of a two-year-old girl, he often talked about the wonderful leave he had enjoyed with her only two months prior. Through grief and many tears, those who were closest to him shared all they could in an effort to let go.

On Monday, August 06, 2007, FOB Kalagush held its first memorial service. Because SGT Harris was assigned to the 202nd MI, the official ceremony was done in Bagram. The ceremony is what many think of—complete with the Soldier's display, colors, twenty-one gun salute and Taps. It is a way for all in the unit to bring closure. As a ceremony, it is mandatory for all to attend, so it is heavy on honoring the Soldier, light on the spiritual. By tradition, there is usually only one ceremony. You can, however, have as many memorial services as you like. These are not mandatory, and they are prepared with the Soldier's faith background in mind. While it too, honors the Soldier, a service brings God more into focus, and encourages the Soldier to think about his mortality in light of eternity. Because it is optional, I assumed that about sixty Soldiers would show up. I miscalculated. Nearly every Soldier on the FOB came to the service.

I stood as the hymn, *Amazing Grace*, played on the bagpipes over our sound system. My message was entitled "Holding out Hope for Eternity" I prayed that it brought comfort and closure to all who heard it.

"And we know that in all things, God works for the good of those who love him, who have been called according to His purpose." (Romans 8:28)

Whenever I read the words in Scripture found in Romans 8:28, the one thing that comes to mind is hope. The hope that no matter what happens, we are never separated from a God that loves us.

One of my favorite movies of all time is "Shawshank Redemption." No doubt most of you have probably seen the movie. It's the story of a man named Andy Dufraine who was wrongfully sentenced for a crime he didn't commit. And after twenty years in the Shawshank prison, he successfully escapes. But during his time at Shawshank, he befriends a man named Red. Red has been denied parole four times and has pretty much given up on the system and no longer has hope. But Andy never gives up hope. It's what keeps him alive and keeps him going in prison. So after he escapes, Andy leaves a note for his friend Red, beckoning him to meet him south of the border in Mexico. In the letter, he writes, "Remember Red. Hope is a good thing. Maybe the best of things. And no good thing ever dies."

So Red makes the decision to commit a crime for the second time in his life — parole violation. He skips town and heads to find his friend in Mexico. As we see the old Trailways bus heading down the highway, Morgan Freeman narrates. "I hope I can make it across the border. I hope to see my friend and shake his hand. I hope the Pacific Ocean is as blue as it has been in my dreams. I hope. I hope."

And so that's my prayer for each of us. That when we leave this service today, we will have hope. Hope that someday, we will see our friend again. Just before the passage that was read today, we read these words. *"For in this hope we were saved. But hope that is seen is no hope at all. Who hopes for what he already has? But if we hope for what we do not yet have, we wait for it patiently."*

So I hold out hope for us today and for the rest of this deployment. My hope is that when we remember SGT Harris, we remember all the good times that we had with him. We remember his smile and his love of life. We remember his servant's heart, and his willingness to serve next to us. And while what we will miss is the future relationship we would have had with Taurean, my hope is that we will see he was a warrior, who gave his life, not needlessly, but selflessly. He gave his life, so that others could live.

I hope that we will remember his family and that we will lift them up in prayer. I pray that we will hold out hope to his baby daughter and have faith that, while we may not yet understand God's plan in all of this, that we will trust He knows what is best, and our hope would be that she grows up to remember that her Daddy paid the ultimate sacrifice so that she could be free.

I hope that whenever we face times like these, our faith will be strengthened and not shattered. I hope that we will come away from this having a deeper love for life, for family and for friends. And that we will never take one minute of life for granted.

But most of all my hope is that, in faith, we will know there is a God who loves us. That we have this hope as an anchor for the soul, firm and secure. We have the hope there is a God who says to each of us, *"I'll always be holding out hope to you. Even when this world breaks your heart in two. When your life is consumed by your fear and your doubts, I'll be holding out hope to you."* It's God who holds us when we grieve, and who comforts us when we mourn.

My prayer for all of us will be what St. Paul says in Romans. *"May the God of hope fill you with all joy and peace as you trust in him, so that you may overflow with hope by the power of the*

Holy Spirit." (Romans 15:12) Remember, hope is a good thing. Maybe the best of things. And no good thing ever dies.

<u>My</u> comfort came at the end of the service. I stood outside the dining facility and as the Soldiers exited, I shook their hands, and put my arm around each one of them. In chaplain school, we learn about the ministry of presence. In Young Life, we called it contact work. Either way, the method is still the same — get to know the people to whom you minister, so that you can someday bring them to the feet of the Savior. I was humbled to realize that with every hand I shook and every hug I gave, I knew every Soldier by face, and by name. "Like a shepherd, he will care for his flock, gathering the lambs in his arms. Hugging them as he carries them, leading them on to good pasture." (Isaiah 40:11, MSG)

Chapter Nine

The Combat Multiplying Chaplain

"When you are about to go into battle, the priest shall come forward and address the army. He shall say, 'Today you are going into battle against your enemies. Do not be fainthearted or afraid; do not be terrified or give way to panic before them. For the Lord your God is the one who goes with you to fight for you against your enemies to give you victory."
(Deuteronomy 20:2-4)

During the basic officer course at chaplain school, we chaplains are constantly told about being a "combat multiplier" on the battlefield. And to be honest, I have really struggled to figure out what that means for me as a chaplain. By the way, it doesn't mean that you go around doing your "times tables" while on combat patrol!

When I was a Military Police Officer, I had no trouble knowing how to be a combat multiplier. It was my responsibility to ensure that I and my Soldiers were proficient in their combat roles and to give them great training opportunities so that when we did deploy, they were a force to be reckoned with. But what about now? I don't carry a weapon so I can't really help in the fighting. Most of the time my assistant and I are "hitching" rides, so it's not like I can drive the HUMVEE in order to free up another shooter. I suppose that when I am on a convoy, I can at least help by being an extra pair of eyes to watch out for possible IEDs or snipers (which I do by the way on every convoy). It's even my desire to become a Combat Lifesaver (like a first responder in the civilian world) and help with first aid. But I have to be honest with you, all of that really doesn't make me a combat **mulitiplier**. I'm simply assisting others.

During the early months of the deployment, I picked back up to read Stephen Mansfield's book, *The Faith of the American Soldier.* I had read it while in chaplain school in preparation for becoming a chaplain. Since then, I had found the book to be even more telling and poignant a read while deployed to a combat zone. One particular chapter is dedicated completely to chaplains and the job we do for Soldiers. (In fact, the book is dedicated to chaplains honoring us as "heroes of the faith who tend the warrior soul.") While I find myself living out the very things Mansfield says in his book, one quote was especially true. Mansfield writes:

The chaplain is described as a "noncombatant." He is not allowed to carry arms, and it is clear that his job is essentially that of a civilian pastor in uniform. In fact, he is not even supposed to go near the fighting. Many chaplains strain at these restrictions and feel that they keep them from doing their jobs. . . . For Millenials at war, the fact that their chaplains cannot "cross the wire," cannot know what they know about being under fire, only makes them less trustworthy. (Mansfield, pg. 100)

I can't tell you how many times I've felt the sting of what Mansfield writes and, for me, how true it is when you are a chaplain in a combat unit. If I had it my way, I would go out on every mission outside the wire of this FOB. I would be right there with them, an assurance of God's strength and protection. And while I had had the great privilege of going on a few missions when I wasn't acting like the circuit riding preacher flying from FOB to FOB, I still wish my command would let me go on more of them.

To my command's credit, however, they do have a good argument to make. Tom often had to remind me that I am not like any other Soldier.

"Don, I'm not saying you don't bring anything to the fight because I don't believe that. You bring a hell of a lot more to the fight than we do when it comes to power. I mean come on, you've got God as your battle buddy for cryin' out loud! But there's only one of you, bro, for the whole battalion. If anything would happen to you out on a mission, there's no telling when we would get another chaplain. Heck, we waited over a year for you to get here!"

I guess I couldn't argue with that. And if I was honest with myself, I had to ask whether I was going out there to relive my days as a combat Soldier, or if I was going out there to minister to Soldiers. Ministry happens everywhere as a chaplain. While a squad is out on a patrol, I could be walking around the FOB talking to Soldiers, preparing for Sunday, or praying.

So I asked the Lord, what was my role in combat? And whenever I stopped to watch our mighty artillery at work, what could I possibly add to that to make it more effective?

Not surprisingly, the answer came in my time with the Lord one morning. I was reading Spurgeon's *Morning and Evening* where he tells the story of Moses praying for Joshua and his men as they fought the Amalekites. You probably know the story:

"So Joshua fought the Amalekites as Moses had ordered, and Moses, Aaron and Hur went to the top of the hill. As long as Moses held up his hands, the Israelites were winning, but whenever he lowered his hands, the Amalekites were winning. When Moses' hands grew tired, they took a stone and put it under him and he sat on it. Aaron and Hur held his hands up—one on one side, one on the other—so that his hands remained steady till sunset. So Joshua overcame the Amalekite army with the sword." (Exodus 17:10-13)

How am I a combat multiplying chaplain? Prayer. So mighty was the prayer of Moses that everything depended on it. As Spurgeon writes, "The petitions of Moses discomfited the enemy more than the fighting of Joshua. Yet both were needed. No, in any conflict, force and fervour, decision and devotion, valour and vehemence must join their forces and all will be well."

How do I add to the battle? I bring the one thing that no weapons forged in fire and steel can prosper against. I pray. I'm often reminded how quickly I forget that prayer is part of the believer's armor, too. "And pray in the Spirit on all occasions with all kinds of prayers and requests. With this in mind, be alert and always keep on praying for all the saints." (Ephesians 6:18) How true that was for me every day as the chaplain over here.

Faithful to His Word on Prayer

On October 19, 2007, I wrote this in my journal:

"Offer to God a sacrifice of thanksgiving, and perform your vows to the Most High, and call upon me in the day of trouble; I will deliver you, and you shall glorify me." (Psalms 50:14-fifteen)

Intel reports say, "Enemy attack imminent and expected. thirty to forty fighters probable." I could sense, Lord, in my spirit that Soldiers are nervous for this one. The threat is very credible. My mission today is to be Moses for Joshua. Keep my arms raised in continual prayer for our Soldiers, Lord.

So Lord, as your Word says, I am calling upon You in the day of trouble. Do what your Word promises — deliver these Soldiers. If there is a battle, bring them through it unscathed. If there is not a battle, let them see that it was You who allowed it. If there is an enemy waiting to attack, open their eyes to see the army of angels that surround the vehicles. (2 Kings 6:16-17)

I trust in your Word, O Lord. Though my flesh and my heart may doubt, I trust in you.

I love you, Sovereign Lord,
Don

Before the Mission

On October 20, 2007, HHB rolled north to the Gandalabuk Village in order to conduct some key leader engagements. As is the custom when I am on the FOB and a patrol is going out, I show up for the mission brief prior to roll-out, and offer encouragement from God's Word and pray for them before they depart. That day I used Psalm 91, the Soldiers' Psalm.

You will not fear the terror of the night, nor the arrow that flies by day, nor the pestilence that stalks in darkness, nor the destruction that wastes at noonday. A thousand may fall at your side, ten thousand at your right hand, but it will not come near you. You will only look with your eyes and see the recompense of the wicked. Because you have made the LORD your dwelling place— the Most High, who is my refuge— no evil shall be allowed to befall you, no plague come near your tent. For he will command his angels concerning you to guard you in all your ways. On their hands they will bear you up, lest you strike your foot against a stone. (Psalms 91:5-12)

I prayed that angels would surround their vehicles and that God would go before them, behind them and be amongst them. I gave each gunner a Shield of Strength dog tag. I gave each MP a prayer coin because I found out from their squad leader that they had not been given one yet. I waited by the gate as each vehicle rolled past calling out to them to be strong and courageous — a phrase that had now become synonymous with my chaplaincy.

But then I did something I had never really done before. Overwhelmed with a desire to send this patrol out in a covering of prayer, I walked over to a bunker that overlooked the valley the patrol was traveling in, and I prayed over them, with my arms raised, until the last vehicle rounded the corner and went out of sight. For those of you who have known me a long time, I don't consider myself to be a prayer warrior. Oh, that I were! I have so many friends whom God has gifted as prayer warriors. And when I am with them, I can sense the power in their prayers. Oh, how I've wanted to be like them! Instead, I go in spurts. I don't pray without ceasing as I ought, but I do know when to pray. That day was one of those days.

For my own walk of faith, I also asked God for reassurance. I prayed that God would show me He was with the patrol, even though I knew in my heart He was. Thanks be to God for His grace in my life, He gave me what I asked for. As I was praying, with my hands raised, I felt a gentle wind at my back. It picked up just as the last vehicle was rounding the corner. Since I was facing the valley and literally standing in a bunker that overlooked the middle of the road, it was as if that wind was moving straight down the valley. A gentle reminder that God was before, amongst and after the patrol.

During the Mission

"Fire mission! Fire mission! Fire Mission!"

The call came down at the gunline. Priority targets laid on, both guns fired just minutes afterwards.

I had just come to the gunline to see how our Soldiers were doing. Because of the probability of enemy contact, both guns were up and the teams were ready. For 2nd platoon, being at FOB Kalagush has not been easy. I have often said that the Soldiers in our battalion who have the highest morale are the ones that are doing their wartime mission. For an artillery gun section, that means the guns are firing in support of troops on the ground. For many of the FOBs, our guns fire every night. For the guns at FOB Kalagush — not so much. Don't get me wrong. As a chaplain, I'm glad when they don't fire. And while it means that boredom may set in for the Soldiers on the gunline, it means that none of our Soldiers are in harm's way.

Obviously, that was not the case this time. Word came down that the patrol was taking small arms and RPGs. The Forward Observer in the convoy had called for fire, and Second Platoon responded. When the last round had been fired from the gun, we waited to get a situation report (SITREP). At times like these, the wait seems like an eternity, when in actuality it is only a few minutes. Still, I don't think I breathed the whole time we were waiting. Finally, the word came back to us. No damage to vehicles or personnel, and the patrol was continuing on with their mission. I congratulated the guys on the gunline for a job well done.

As I walked on, I started to feel like I had failed in my mission. Why had there been contact with the enemy? Wasn't God with them? Why did He allow the enemy to fire?

You will not fear the terror of the night, nor the arrow that flies by day, nor the pestilence that stalks in darkness, nor the destruction that wastes at noonday. A thousand may fall at your side, ten thousand at your right hand, but it will not come near you.

No damage to vehicles or personnel. God reassured me that He was with them. Yet, even though I tried to focus on other things, I couldn't stop thinking about the patrol. So I just did what seemed natural — I went back to the bunker facing the valley. I told God I wasn't leaving until I saw the vehicles coming back. So for the next few hours, I stood watch in the bunker. For me, it was a precious time with the Lord. I read and reread Psalm 91. I prayed that God would continue to protect them just like He promised in His Word. I raised my arms and called out to God, straining my eyes to see the first glimpse of any vehicle. Gradually, I started to grow tired. Was God still there? When would they be coming back? Selfishly, I needed to know that He was still holding this patrol in the palm of His hands.

No sooner had I prayed that prayer, than God graciously reassured me. Closing my eyes, I felt a gentle breeze blow directly on my face. The exact opposite from what had happened that morning. As I stood there, the breeze gradually increased in strength. Tears streamed down my face because I knew God was answering my prayers. Even though it was almost completely dark, I heard the familiar sound of Humvee engines in the distance. The patrol was on its way back and God was leading the way.

After the Mission

As the Humvees rolled through the gate, I stood by waving to each of them, thanking God for their safe return. The mission was a success, and all the Soldiers were doing well. Not surprisingly, none of the Soldiers seemed too traumatized by the attack either. Many of the Soldiers came up to me saying they never felt afraid because they knew God and His angels were protecting them.

After a quick debriefing, CPT Donatelle let everyone go and refit, commending them for their efforts that day. Over dinner, Tom gave me the "play-by-play" of what transpired. After leaving FOB Kalagush, the unit moved north as planned. Once the first group of trucks was in position to cover movement, the second group of trucks moved forward. As the second group of trucks was completing its first bound to the first group of trucks' location, they received indirect fire. The convoy was ambushed by indirect fire (IDF) stemming from two different locations. The first round impacted in front of the platoon leader's vehicle, right next to the Afghan National Police truck. The second round impacted between the platoon leader's vehicle and 1st squad's vehicle as they were pushing through the "kill zone". The third round impacted to the south of 1st squad's vehicle. The fourth and fifth round impacted to the north of them. The sixth and final round exploded just above the river to their east. The impacts for the IDF rounds were all in the same general area. The platoon also observed small arms fire stemming from the enemy positions. Still, the end result was the same. Even though the rounds impacted all around them, not one did any damage.

One of the MPs whom I had given a coin to before the mission, stopped me after dinner that evening.

"Hey Chaps!" he said running up to me with a big smile. "Thanks for giving me this coin today. I keep it in the pocket right over my heart!" Patting his pocket for good measure.

I smiled. "Sergeant," I said, putting my arm over his shoulders. "That coin is more than just something to keep in your pocket like a good luck charm. It's to remind you that there are literally thousands of people praying for you each every day."

"I know that now, sir," he said with confidence. "See you Sunday in chapel!"

Somehow, I figured more than just the regular attendees would show up for chapel that Sunday. I was right. That Sunday, our little tent was packed. And when it came time for offering praises and prayer requests, many stood up to thank God for protecting them on the mission.

When he calls to me, I will answer him; I will be with him in trouble; I will rescue him and honor him. (Psalms 91:15)

Before every mission, the Soldiers would gather around for a prayer to ask the Lord for protection, strength and courage.

Chapter Ten

Three Simple Questions

"Whatever you do, work at it with all your heart as working for the Lord, not for men, since you know that you will receive an inheritance from the Lord as a reward. It is the Lord Christ you are serving. (Colossians 3:23-24)

As soon as we arrived in country, our battalion commander, LTC Steve Maranian, gave us three questions that we as leaders needed to ask ourselves every day. He told us that if we could adequately answer them at the end of each day, then we will have done our job. Three simple questions:

1. What have you done to ensure the safe firing of every projectile out of your section's howitzer?

2. What have you done to improve the quality of life for your Soldiers?

3. What have you done for the good people of Afghanistan today?

Obviously, not all of these questions could be fully answered each and every day, but as I traveled around the battlefield, I definitely saw them as a great barometer for the Soldiers of the 4-319th. And as I was flying from FOB Lybert to FOB Khogyani one day, I had the chance to reflect on the awesome way in which the Soldiers up at Lybert did that so well.

Safe Firing

"Fire Mission! Fire Mission!"

The call over the radio jolted me out of bed. I was staying in the VIP quarters at Lybert which was right next to the gun section. Incidentally, to call my room a VIP room would probably be a bit of an overstatement. The room was four feet by eight feet with a cot and some shelves in it. Still, I was honored that they considered me a "VIP" and put me up in what was perhaps the best room on the FOB.

Although I didn't get right out of bed (the mission came down in the middle of the night), I heard the section go through their meticulous drill of setting the gun on azimuth, getting the type of round and fuse combination together for the mission, the section chief yelling out commands to each of his Soldiers — the ammo bearer, the radio operator, the "round stuffer" (what I like to call him anyway!), the gunner, and the Soldier who pulls the lanyard. Only after the chief has checked and rechecked all the steps will he point to the gunner for him to say, "Fire!"

Knowing that I wasn't going to get much sleep for a while, I decided to get up and "see what all the racket was about." So I made my way over to the howitzer where the gun section was getting ready to fire another mission. As I looked out on the horizon, I saw it was lit up almost as bright as day. The gun section was firing illumination rounds. When I asked the chief why they were firing illumination, he let me know that they often do it to deny the enemy movement under the cover of darkness. Likewise, it gives the forward observers and infantry scouts illumination to look down certain avenues of approach for the enemy. And in this terrain, any valley coming out of Pakistan is a likely avenue of approach!

"Just trying to make it safe for our boys out there, sir!" SSG Greenjack said.

A tall, wiry man, this was the chief's fourth deployment — each one of them a year or more. There was no doubt in my mind that he knew what it took to safely put rounds down range in support of our fellow Soldiers on patrol.

"Sir, you mind if I ask you a question?" he asked.

"Not at all, sergeant," I smiled in reply. "What's on your mind?"

"Well, isn't this hard for you?" he asked quizzically.

"I'm not sure I understand what you are asking me," I said, a bit confused.

"I mean, you know, here you are, a man of the cloth. You come out to see us whenever you can and hope to bring encouragement — which you do, by the way," he said reassuringly, as if hoping not to offend me. "But then again, you are a part of a combat unit. Our job is to close with and destroy the enemy and you come down to the gunline to watch. Is God OK with that?"

I think I know now how Nehemiah must have felt when he was asked by the king what was troubling him. As the cupbearer to the king, he needed to choose his words wisely, for they could have been his last. And while it was by no means that drastic for me, I still did what Nehemiah did before he answered the king — I prayed (see Nehemiah 2:4). I wanted to be able to answer the chief in a way that brought honor to the Lord, but not come across like an arrogant know-it-all on spiritual matters.

"Well, sergeant, do you think anybody with a seminary degree could do the job of a chaplain?" I asked.

Thinking about it for a moment, he responded, "No, I guess not."

"I don't think so either. You see, the reason why we have chaplains in the Army is because we are expected to be Soldiers right alongside you all," I explained, as I pulled out my pocket new testament. I turned to 1 Corinthians 9:19-23:

I am not anyone's slave. But I have become a slave to everyone, so that I can win as many people as possible. When I am with the Jews, I live like a Jew to win Jews. They are ruled by the Law of Moses, and I am not. But I live by the Law to win them. And when I am with people who are not ruled by the Law, I forget about the Law to win them. Of course, I never really forget about the law of God. In fact, I am ruled by the law of Christ. When I am with people whose faith is weak, I live as they do to win them. I do everything I can to win everyone I possibly can. I do all this for the good news, because I want to share in its blessings.

"You see, chief," I explained. "I am a Soldier in a combat unit just like you. And so I want to be wherever you guys are. If I were to rephrase this passage, I would say, 'when I am with the Soldiers, I live like a Soldier to win Soldiers.'"

The chief looked out to the horizon as he thought about what I had just told him. "So, you come down to the gunline to be like us in order to bring us to God?"

"Well, I go wherever my Soldiers are. And as their chaplain, my job is to represent the best that God has for them," I said, smiling. "So when there's a fire mission, I want to be on the gunline when it happens." Then I winked at him and said, "And I think that's exactly where God wants me to be."

Improving Quality of Life

This was now my second trip up to the FOB, and whenever I returned to Kalagush, I would always comment on how difficult a job the guys up at Lybert have. In fact, I can safely say that, even though they have been working hard and have stayed motivated since arriving there in May, their fun meter was about pegged. Now I think it was starting to get old. The hard part about me writing that statement was that we still had eleven months to go. And unfortunately, the worst was yet to come.

Because Lybert is about 7,000 feet above sea level, they could expect to get the worst that an Afghan winter brings their way. The unit we replaced shared pictures with the battery of eight foot snow drifts and doing patrols with snow shoes and crampons. To be honest, once the war is over and commerce continues to grow, FOB Lybert has the potential to be a winter lover's paradise. It would not take much work at all to build it into a ski resort! In all seriousness though, the winter could prove to be more than our Soldiers were bargaining for when they signed on to come over here.

In addition, for many of our Soldiers, this was their third and fourth deployment. One Soldier that came in for counseling while at Lybert told me that in the last six years, he calculated he has been with his wife and son a total of only eighteen months.

"I can't do this anymore, chaplain," he said, his lips quivering and his eyes welling up with tears. "I just want to go home. I'm almost ready to do something stupid so that they will have to kick me out. It's just not worth it anymore."

As I sat and listened, many thoughts came to mind of what I could say to him:

Remember that you are doing this for your country. . .

Before you know it, you'll be back home. . .

Doing something drastic to get kicked out of the army will only make things worse. . .

I could have said those things, but I didn't. They weren't what he needed to hear. And to be honest, I found myself at a loss for words. After all, these Soldiers have more than done their service to our nation. They raised their hands to serve when others chose not to. They've come to fight and win our nation's wars. And for the most part, they almost never complain. These men and women are some of the most resilient I have ever known. They inspire me and I am humbled by their selfless service.

So, too, it is with their families back home. Though we live a somewhat "bachelor life" over here, our spouses are single parents. Getting the kids ready for school, helping them with their homework when they get home, ensuring dinner is on the table, shuttling them to soccer games, play practice and home-coming dances. For some spouses, this is their third and fourth time doing the single parent thing. They are heroes as well.

And when I can't say anything, when I can't find the right words to give comfort, I am left with only the promise that I will be praying for them and seek to reassure them that God is with them even in these dark times. And yet I know that is enough because Jesus Christ is sufficient.

Not surprisingly, my quiet times with the Lord seemed to constantly reveal just such a sentiment. In the fall, I began reading 2 Corinthians, and was amazed to find it so apropos for what we were experiencing in Afghanistan. In fact, I was so struck by its accurate depiction of what we are going through here, that I read the passage in several different versions. *The Message* puts it as plainly as any:

> *We don't want you in the dark, friends, about how hard it was when all this came down on us in Asia province. It was so bad we didn't think we were going to make it. We felt like we'd been sent to death row, that it was all over for us. As it turned out, it was the best thing that could have happened. Instead of trusting in our own strength or wits to get out of it, we were forced to trust God totally—not a bad idea since he's the God who raises the dead! And he did it, rescued us from certain doom. And he'll do it again, rescuing us as many times as we need rescuing. You and your prayers are part of the rescue operation—I don't want you in the dark about that either. I can see your faces even now, lifted in praise for God's deliverance of us, a rescue in which your prayers played such a crucial part. (2 Corinthians 1:8-11, MSG)*

I was overcome with emotion when I read this passage because it again reminded me of the truth about our God — that He is sovereign, and that He is good. My prayer remained throughout the fifteen months that this deployment would cause all of the Soldiers which I shepherd to place their trust in God totally and completely — certain that He will rescue us from all adversity, be it direct or indirect attacks, combat stress, family strife or marital challenges.

Even amidst all this separation, multiple deployments, and extreme hardships, the Soldiers of Alpha Battery at Lybert surprised me with their resilience and positive attitude. The FOB "mayor", SSG Shwener, gave me the grand tour of all the projects which they were working on in order to fully winterize the camp. He showed me the new "stone and mud" barracks that they were building. They would be fitted inside with insulation and plywood. He showed me the foundation of the new hardstand dining facility which would be finished in a month to replace the tent they were now using. He told me about the plan to bring in a rock crusher so they could lay gravel where all the dirt was in hopes that that would alleviate the "slip and slide" affect which will inevitably come with the first snow. As I listened to him talk, I could see what pride he was taking in his work and how much he was hoping to improve the living conditions for his Soldiers.

"I just wish there was one thing I could improve," he said, disappointed.

"Oh? And what would that be, sergeant?" I asked.

"I wish I could bring in something to give these guys better connectivity to the outside world," he said pointing over to the little tent that served as the Internet café for the Soldiers. "But the café is down more than it is up," he explained. "Most of the time, Soldiers come out of the tent with a sullen and angry look on their face. I always know that they have had no luck getting online to check email or call home. And don't even think about trying to get online to chat with your wife!"

"Well, what would it take to make that happen up here?" I asked.

The young sergeant thought about this for a little while. "I suppose if we could get an MWR satellite up here like the other FOBs have, it would make things a whole lot better," he said matter-of-factly. "But we have already been told it probably won't happen. It's just logistically too hard. We hear that a lot, and it's pretty discouraging when there are others in Afghanistan who actually have Internet in their rooms."

He was referring to larger FOBs like Bagram where the Soldiers are able to purchase Internet and cable for their rooms at about fifty dollars a month. I could definitely see his point. There did seem to be an equity problem there.

The sergeant looked me straight in the eye and said, "Getting something like that up here would improve morale on this FOB by five hundred percent!"

I told him I didn't think I could promise anything, but I would see what I could do.

Incidentally, as the year went on, the quality of life greatly improved. They built a hardstand dining facility complete with griddle for eggs made to order. They got a new and improved gym with state of the art equipment. And finally, they did get the satellite hookup so the MWR computers ran faster and more efficiently. Lybert still wasn't palatial, but it was bearable.

Helping the Locals

Sean Hipp sat across from me on the deck of the FOB's aid station. A captain who came into the Army to pay for medical school, CPT Hipp specializes in family medicine and pediatrics.

Sipping on a coffee cup with a label that reads, "Does anybody know where the heck Ausfahrt Germany is?" (exit signs on the Autobahn in Germany all say "Ausfahrt" which means "exit"), he is the quintessential Army doctor. Attending medical school at UNC, Sean loved practicing medicine and loved the Army as well.

"It just seemed like the perfect fit," he says, taking a long pull from his coffee cup. "But when I deployed to Afghanistan, I didn't think I would be practicing pediatrics. That is, until I came to Lybert."

Originally stationed at FOB Naray (renamed FOB Bostick after Major Tom Bostick was killed), Dr. Hipp was assigned to the forward surgical team there. Most of his work was with injured Soldiers, and every four weeks or so, the FST would send up a doc to Lybert for a couple of weeks to treat the Soldiers and the locals, then rotate them back to Naray. But when it came time for Sean's rotation, he came up to Lybert and never left. For of all the FOBs in theater, Lybert's aid station serves more like a medical clinic for the local villages than any other. Ninety-eight percent of its patients are local nationals, and of those ninety-eight percent, nearly forty percent are children.

"The villagers here simply don't have the medical facilities that we have," he explained. "Most simply use home remedies like packing wounds with mud or covering burns with mascara." (You read that right, by the way. These people seem to think that mascara has healing qualities because of how beautiful it can accentuate a woman's eyes!)

"Most adults will simply live with the pain if they can't get to a doctor—and they will do so for days on end," he continued. "But with their children, it is a different story. They want to do anything they can to have their children grow up with a fighting chance."

The next morning, I got to see what Dr. Hipp was talking about first hand. After enjoying a great breakfast (the food being one of the few things that every Soldier agrees is a plus being stationed at Lybert), I sat looking out over the beautiful valley. Even though it's a remote place, I never grew tired of the incredible landscape which God created here. After my time with the Lord, I glanced over to the aid station deck. I saw a father with no less than eight children sitting around him. I walked over to the deck.

The Afghan father smiled and, holding his baby daughter in one arm, offered his other hand in greeting. He shook my hand and then placed his hand over his heart as a sign of good faith. From the interpreter, I learned that this father had two wives and all of the children with him were his. He and the children had walked over two hours to come to the aid station. In his arms, he was holding his three-month old daughter who was throwing a pretty good fit. Dr. Hipp had told him to bring her in for a well-baby checkup.

I gestured to him with my arms out to see if he would let me hold her. He smiled widely and happily handed her over. Dressed in a little gold burqa which covered everything but her beautiful face, she looked at me with big brown eyes. She started to cry again, so, naturally, I did what I had done with all of my own daughters, and placed her head on my shoulder and began to pat her back. Within minutes, she was asleep, and I was in heaven. For the next fifteen minutes or so, I rocked this little baby, singing worship songs in her ear, making funny faces to her brothers and sisters, and simply enjoying the love of this Afghan family. The highlight of the day for the kids was getting a picture taken with their new friend from the US Army.

Three questions. Three simple things to do. One ensured we honor our agreement to be in this country and minimize all collateral damage from firing our howitzers. The other ensured that our Soldiers can make it to the finish line even though we were there fifteen months. And, finally, the other ensures that families like the one that came to Lybert's aid station, will be able to see their children grow up healthy and free.

The children of one Afghan family that walked over two days to get to the aid station at Lybert

Chapter Eleven

The Boys of Bella

"Even though I walk through the valley of the shadow of
death, I will fear no evil." (Psalm 23)

November's rounds of battlefield circulation proved to be
the most challenging ones to date. Over three weeks'
time, SPC Marshall and I would visit Paruns, COP Blessing,
and a little outpost named Bella. All of the places were very
remote with limited communications and a high probability
of enemy contact. Before my trip, I spent much time in prayer
preparing my heart for what lie ahead.

Journal Entry, November 2, 2007
"Therefore I will boast all the more gladly of my weaknesses, so that
the power of Christ may rest upon me. For the sake of Christ, then, I am
content with weaknesses, insults, hardships, persecutions, and calamities.
For when I am weak, then I am strong." (2 Corinthians 12:9b-10)

Lord Jesus,

This is kind of really where I must "put my money where my mouth
is," I guess. I leave tomorrow for another trip of battlefield circulation and
I confess to You that I am more nervous this go around than ever before.

Paruns, Blessing, Bella, Lybert — they all have the potential of bad things happening there.

But I hate being scared, Lord! I am the one who preaches to be strong and courageous! I know that You use me to encourage Soldiers and to show them that You are real and with them. And yet, I can't help but have this gnawing feeling in the pit of my stomach that something could happen.

When I read Your Word today, Lord, I find myself asking, "Am I <u>really</u> content?" Am I content that one of my weaknesses is fear of the unknown? Am I content when I experience insults like the ones that atheist Soldiers hurl my way as they drive out the gate for a mission? Am I content with the hardship of living out of a rucksack for most of the next three weeks? Am I content with the calamities that may come on this trip? In my flesh, I confess I am content with none of it.

And yet, that is exactly the way You designed it. If I must experience insults, it is for the sake of Christ (2 Corinthians 2:14-16). If I must endure hardships it is for the sake of Christ (2 Timothy 2:3). If I must face calamities (which I see in Greek literally means "narrowness of place" – pretty much defines the size of FOB Bella and Lybert!) it is for the sake of Christ (2 Corinthians 6:3-4), so that all may see that Your power is made perfect in weakness and the Gospel is true for everyone, everywhere.

On my own, I am a coward. But called by You, Lord, to carry the gospel, I am bold, strong, steadfast, and powerful because I do this ministry in <u>Your</u> strength and in <u>Your</u> power! (Colossians 1:28-29)

Lord Jesus, protect your servants — me and Marshall. Keep us safely in the shadow of your wings. Let us boldly proclaim the gospel, for it is fruitful labor for us! Thank you for my weaknesses, that your power would be made perfect in me.

Only by your grace Lord,
Don

The trip started out with us traveling with the Provincial Recovery Team from Kalagush to Paruns. It is the capital of the Nuristan district. Honestly, if I didn't know that I was in Afghanistan, I would have thought that I was back home in Montana! The governor of Nuristan knows this as well and, since he spent many years living and working in the United States, he has great plans for Paruns to become the tourist capital of Afghanistan. Sounds pretty crazy now, but given twenty to twenty-five years, I believe that dream may, in fact, become a reality.

The PRT dropped us off at Command Outpost (COP) Blessing a few days later and we immediately went over to the gunline. Because it is away from the rest of the COP, the gun platoon pretty much kept to themselves. They had their own little chow hall as well as full bathroom and laundry. Morale for these guys was extremely high because they were constantly doing their wartime mission. Security reasons won't allow me to tell you exactly how many rounds they have fired, but suffice it to say it was in the thousands. They were, by far, the busiest platoon in our battalion which speaks volumes about the enemy situation in their Area of Operation (AO).

As always, my most favorite thing whenever I went there was to conduct a gunline worship service. Each time we went to Blessing, the platoon sergeant set up our altar on the grill that they had built near the gunline. (Marshall often joked and called this "Grillin' with God"!) Most of the Soldiers would come out to give thanks to our Lord for keeping them safe, singing praise songs, and breaking bread together. Our time at Blessing was always, well, a blessing!

At the next resupply, Marshall and I headed out to Bella. The day prior, I had gone up to the company's command post (CP) to get a brief on the enemy situation out there as well as call the platoon leader, 1LT Matthew Ferrera, to let him know that we were coming and that, hopefully, we could sleep in one of the B-Huts rather than under the stars. Everything was set for our trip.

When we arrived, however, I can definitely say that we received a less than warm welcome. I guess in some ways I couldn't blame them. After all, none of these guys were from our battalion, and I would imagine that the platoon sergeant (who, by the way, had no idea we were coming and the platoon leader was out on mission) simply took it as a gesture by the brigade to send out a chaplain to their little camp because they haven't had one in a while. There must have been a part of him that felt like, "What? We're not good enough for our own battalion chaplain to come out to us?" But as we talked, I told him how Chaplain Schnarr, their battalion chaplain, was hands down, the busiest chaplain in the brigade, and it is next to impossible for him to hit all of his FOBs all the time. (One time I asked him how long it would take to get to each FOB, or COP as was the case with Bella and Blessing, in his AO at least once. He told me six to eight weeks.) Needless to say, after we had to find our own place to sleep, I remember thinking to myself that this was going to be a long five days. I even started to wonder why God would have sent me here in the first place.

In Young Life, we learn that there are three phases of contact work — being seen by kids, talking to kids, and doing something with kids. I've pretty much kept to that same philosophy since becoming a chaplain. I strongly believe in "earning the right to be heard" so I find myself going into "contact work" mode whenever I begin a new phase of ministry. As a result, my first hour or so on the COP was simply Marshall and me walking around being seen and talking to the Soldiers there. This was, however, a much different environment than Kalagush or Blessing. For one, we were required to keep our flak jackets on at all times. Because of the location of the COP and the constant enemy threat, no one left their hooch without wearing their vest. Second, the COP was tiny. Smaller than a football field, it consisted of a few B-Huts, a dining facility (another B-Hut) and an LZ (Landing Zone) for a helicopter. That's it. No running water, no latrines, nothing. So, contact work was pretty easy to do since the COP was so small. (I have since learned that COPs and FOBs have size differentials to them, hence why Bella is a COP. I know, it's a lot of acronyms to remember!) I quickly learned the names of those who were at Bella. The rest of the platoon was out on a patrol mission. They had left the day before to go over the mountain to a Shura (elders) meeting and were not expected back until nightfall. That would soon change less than three hours later . . .

Standing next to the mortar pit, I was talking to the guys in the mortar section. All of them were between the ages of eighteen and twenty-one. I was awed at their maturity level, their dedication to their job, and the belief in what they were doing. One of the Soldiers, SPC Farris, was from New Jersey. We immediately hit it off because I told him about growing up in Connecticut. He told me he was a Yankees fan. I let him know I was a Red Sox fan. We ribbed each other about our teams and laughed about being over here for yet another World Series which, by the way, the Red Sox won!

At one point, I was about to ask him about the 120mm mortar, when I noticed that there seemed to be a lot of commotion going on. Soldiers were running to positions, leaders were talking on radios and barking out orders. I felt a little uncomfortable because I didn't exactly know what was going on.

Just then, the mortar section leader ran out of the mortar team's hooch and announced to the team, "Get ready for a fire mission guys!" he yelled. "The OP (observation post) has seen enemy moving in the mountains above us to the south and they are heading towards our scouts."

The section sprang into action. For the most part, it's pretty much like watching the boys on the big guns. One guy goes to get the round, the other sets the gun. The team leader takes down the coordinates, and the section leader verifies them before firing. The main difference is that on a Howitzer, the Soldier attaches a lanyard from behind the gun to trigger the firing pin. For a mortar, you hang the round over the tube and then drop it in.

"Hang it!" the leader barked. The mortarman hung the round over the tube. Each round weighs over forty pounds, so these guys are all built like brick outhouses!

"Fire!"

He dropped the round and we waited about ten seconds to see it land at the crest of the mountain. As soon as the round impacted, we started to hear small arms fire. The OP above Bella opened up with its machine guns as did the guard posts on the perimeter of the base. Word came down from the platoon TOC (tactical operations center) that the squad which was on its way back from the Shura meeting was caught in an ambush, and the scouts that were covering their movement from the mountain above Bella were about to be overrun. Still over next to the mortar pit, Marshall and I got in place behind some barriers. I placed Marshall online with the other Soldiers. He, along with several Soldiers, returned fire on the small team of anti-coalition militiamen (ACM) coming down the mountain towards the scouts.

What transpired next almost feels like it defied time. I remember looking at my watch before and after the attack, and over an hour would pass — but it seemed like a blur of only ten minutes.

As the OP and the Soldiers of the COP continued to fire on the anti-coalition militia (ACM), the mortars continued to fire rounds at the mountain. At one point, Marshall looked over to me and yelled, "Chaplain, you need to get inside one of the B-Huts!" I simply shook my head, and he could tell from my face that I wasn't going anywhere.

"I'm fine Marshall!" I yelled reassuringly. "I'm right where I need to be! These boys right here are in the fight, and their chaplain needs to be right next to them, not hunkered down underneath a bunk!" No sooner had I said that than an RPG landed over our heads near the entrance to the COP.

Once he knew he wasn't going to get me to go inside, he at least made sure I was behind a large Hesco barrier (a sand filled barrier that is about five feet high and four feet thick) at the back of the mortar pit. He told me to stay down, and he high crawled back over to his fighting position with the other Soldiers. Having never been in a fire fight before, Marshall defined "baptism by fire." But he was awesome, and I was never more proud of my chaplain's assistant than I was at that very moment.

Each time the guys hung a round, I would encourage them. "That's it guys, stay in the fight!" I would call out. "Hang another one! You're doing great! Those scouts are going to end up owing their lives to you! Come on! The Lord is with you!"

Several RPGs landed just outside the wire. Overhead, our boys at Blessing started dropping rounds near the ambush site. Four, five, six rounds whistled in as the gunline "fired for effect." Minutes later, two F-15s, or "fast movers" as they are nicknamed by the Joes on the ground, fired several precision guided missiles down the valley. The sound was deafening.

Soon, the firing died down. We got word that the scouts had escaped by a different route. It was unclear from our position whether or not the fighters had been killed or just retreated, but for the most part, Bella was out of danger.

I wish the same could have been said for the patrol coming back. On their way back to Bella, the squad, along with the platoon leader got caught in a multi-directional ambush. A well positioned enemy force attacked the patrol on a trail in the mountains with small arms, machine guns and RPGs. When it was all over, the whole squad was either wounded or killed.

Earlier, I questioned why God had placed me at Bella. I know now that I will never question God's providence or sovereign timing ever again. Ministry to the Soldiers at Bella took everything I had ever learned as a chaplain in chaplain school, a staff member in Young Life, or a Navigator at West Point. And although I could tell countless stories of my time spent with the boys of Bella over those next few days, there are three that I will tell.

The Squad Leader

The young staff sergeant ran into the aid station where Marshall and I were staying. He called out to one of the medics.

"Let's go, man!" he bellowed. "The squad outside the wire needs us!"

This young squad leader was a true infantryman. He had gathered up a team of Soldiers and gave them a brief before heading out. As nightfall approached, those who were wounded had called back for a MEDEVAC to get them and the KIA out. Because of the precarious nature of their location, the MEDEVAC birds were going to have to extract them. This required some assistance. They were heading out to the ambush site to get the rest of the wounded up and in those helicopters. It would prove to be a very long night, but this small squad of Soldiers did their job beautifully. Once the rest of the QRF arrived on scene, they were able to come back and refit.

I stood by the gate of the base while they came back in and greeted them as they entered. I smiled and said, "Hey guys, great job out there. Welcome back. Been praying for you."

The squad leader was the last to come through the gate. Sweaty and tired, he looked like he had been through a lot. Dropping his assault pack on the ground, he sat down on a rock just inside the wire. I walked over to him. I could tell it had been tough for him.

"Hey sergeant," I said patting him on the knee as I sat down next to him. "You did a great job out there."

He shook his head in protest and quietly replied, "Not enough, sir. Not enough. I should have been out there with them."

As we talked, I learned that the squad that got ambushed was actually his squad. He had gone back to Blessing to pick up some funds to pay the local nationals who work at Bella picking up trash, helping out in the dining facility and doing small jobs around the base. It is, what we call in the military, an extra duty. He wasn't on the patrol because he was doing a different part of his job; one that on any other day, he would have thought nothing of. In fact, if the ambush had never happened, I dare say he probably would have enjoyed the fact that he was getting to go back to some form of civilization outside of Bella. Blessing has a great chow hall, hot showers, and an awesome gym. Every Soldier enjoys coming back to headquarters for a little refit.

But niceties are short lived when faced with the guilt that, as a leader, you were not with your men at a critical time in battle. That is the time you train for as a squad. It's why squad leaders pound crew drills and individual tactics into their Soldiers' heads. The weight of that guilt was probably more overbearing for him than the actual combat would have been had he been there with them.

Every muscle in his face convulsed as he gritted his teeth and pounded his fists onto his thighs. He cried out, "I should have been there with them, sir! I wish I could have been there!"

He buried his head into his hands and began to sob. I put my arms around him and drew him into my chest as I started to cry as well. "I know you do, son," I said reassuringly. "I know you do."

"But for some reason, you weren't. There's a verse in the Bible that says, 'In his heart a man plans his course, but the Lord directs his steps (Proverbs 16:9).' What that says to me is that, as hard as it is right now for you to understand, God did not want you on that mission. You are alive today because of that. And the greatest gift you can give your squad is to continue to lead." He looked up at me with swollen eyes as I continued.

"I've been talking to the guys back here while you were out at the ambush site, and they all said that if anything was to happen to you, that would be the end of the platoon. You give them hope, sergeant," I said smiling. "You are a source of strength for this platoon! And right now, these guys need you to reassure them that they are going to get through this. Now I'm not telling you to not grieve, because I'm grieving with you. But I am asking you to continue to give these guys hope." With that, I asked if I could pray for him, and we both prayed together that God would give him the strength he would need in the weeks to come.

In the days that would follow, this squad leader seemed to know what he needed to do. I overheard him talking on the phone to one of his guys that had been wounded, giving encouragement and telling him how proud he was of him. I watched as he diligently went through the belongings of the Soldiers who had been killed, meticulously preparing them to be sent home to their family. During our chapel service, he asked for prayers for the families of the Soldiers that were killed, one in particular whose wife was due with their first child in February. This young squad leader grew up in those few days, and I think his faith grew as well.

The Scout

"Hey chaplain?" a voice called out to me in the darkness. I was on my way back from the "outhouse" late one night. Because of the enemy threat, we can't use white light on our flashlights and have to use a red lens. It works OK as long as you watch where you are going. His voice startled me a little.

"Yeah, man. What's up?" I replied.

"I was wondering if you might be able to come by my hooch tomorrow. I wanted you to look over the prayer that I am going to say at our guys' memorial ceremony. Plus, I'd like to talk to you about some personal things." I told him I would come by right after breakfast.

The next morning, I went to see this Soldier. He was a team leader with the scouts and had been providing overwatch on the patrol coming back when it was ambushed. He saw everything unfold, not to mention the threat of the enemy trying to make their way down to their position.

"It was pretty chaotic for a while," he said, looking down at the floor. "I wasn't sure if this was going to be it for us or not. A couple of those mortar rounds hit dangerously close to our position. We couldn't make our way back to the switchback, so we had to traverse down the steep mountain." He laughed and added, "I pretty much did the butt slide the whole way down!"

Then his face got serious again as he looked up at me when he said, "The mortars saved our lives, sir. Which is why I wanted to talk to you." He handed me the prayer he had written in honor of his buddies. One of the Soldiers who died he had known since basic training. The prayer was beautiful in its simplicity — so real and genuine. Most definitely from the heart.

I handed it back to him and said, "This is a great prayer sergeant. I wouldn't change a thing. It's straight from your heart and I'm sure your buddy would be honored to know that you wrote it and gave it at his memorial."

Again the sergeant stared down at the floor. He shook his head and said, "That's just it, sir. I don't know if I'm worthy to read this prayer or even say it for that matter. I would feel like a hypocrite if I did." His eyes started to well up with tears when he looked up at me to say, "Being out there, knowing I might die, made me think of all the bad things I've done in my life. It's been a long time since I've really prayed or even given a rip about God. I remember hearing somewhere that God doesn't hear the prayers of a sinful man, and I have to be honest when I say to you, I'm a sinful man."

I put my hand on his shoulder and looked him straight in the eyes. "Well what would you like to do about that sergeant?" I asked.

He simply replied, "Make it right. I want to be right with God, sir. I feel like I need to give my confession and recommit my life to Jesus."

I opened my pocket New Testament and showed him 1 John 1:9 and read to him, "If we confess our sins, he is faithful and just to forgive us our sins and purify us from all unrighteousness."

So over the next fifteen minutes, this young Soldier confessed his sins. It was like seeing a weight come off his shoulders. We then sat on his bunk and prayed together. His desire was to get back to God — to live his life for Christ and be assured of his salvation.

In wartime, we often hear stories about Soldiers who say, "God, if you get me through this battle unharmed, I will serve you the rest of my life." We call it foxhole religion. Coming face to face with their mortality in the light of eternity, Soldiers want to know that if they die they will be with God. More often than not, the prayer and the commitment are short lived. So as I said goodbye to this sergeant, I gave him a pocket New Testament and encouraged him to start reading it every day. He told me he would, and I planned on getting with him the next time I came to Bella.

The Survivor

Just before I left to head back to Bagram to continue our travels, the first sergeant asked me if I would take a couple of wallets with me and drop them off at the hospital to the guys who were wounded. They were scheduled to fly to Landstuhl the next day. I told him that I would be honored to. However, as is often the case in a theater of operations, patients who are headed back to the rear usually go on the "next thing smokin'" back to Germany. As a result, the two Soldiers flew out about six hours before I arrived in BAF. Not wanting to keep two wallets with money and identification on my person, I decided to go to their company's supply office at BAF. After I introduced myself, the supply sergeant smiled and said, "Oh yeah, you're the chaplain that was out at the COP with these guys. We heard all about you. Thanks for being there with them."

I smiled back and said, "The honor has been all mine, sergeant. Because of this trip, I have come to see how God truly orchestrates our lives in a perfect plan. I'm awed that He would choose me to be there for such a time as this."

He nodded affirmatively then replied, "Yes sir, God is pretty awesome. Well, what brings you over here, sir?"

I went on to tell him that I had these two wallets and needed to give them to him to inventory and secure until they could find a way to get them to the Soldiers. He assured me that he would do that. Then he looked at the name of one of the Soldiers and smiled. "SPC White." This Soldier was one of the heroes of the ambush, and he relayed the story to me.

As the platoon leader's RTO (Radio operator), White was on the patrol right next to 1LT Ferrera. When the ambush started, he was knocked unconscious by an RPG receiving shrapnel to his face. When he came to, he found that his platoon leader was dead and his radio destroyed. There was firing going on all around him. He low crawled over to the Marine who was in charge of the Afghan Soldiers on patrol with them. When he got there, he found that he was dead as well, but his radio was still working. He put it on his back and called in the ambush along with a sitrep (situation report) to Bella. Because he was able to make contact, the command post was able to call for fire and provide air support for the Soldiers on the ground. Because of the wounds to his face, he faded in and out of conscious several times. Each time he awoke, however, he made it over to his buddies and provided first aid to them. There is a great chance that several of the seven who were wounded might not have lived if he hadn't performed life-saving measures.

Listening to this story, I wished I had been able to meet this survivor, this great Soldier. He is a hero in every sense of the word. It brought back memories of reading about the young men of World War II in Tom Brokaw's *The Greatest Generation*. So many have thought that they are no more. But those people have never met the Boys of Bella. Each one of them is, and forever will be, warriors and heroes to me.

"Endure hardship with us like a good Soldier of Christ Jesus." (2 Timothy 2:3)

How that verse would ring truer than ever in my mind from now on.

As I got off the Chinook at Kalagush, twenty-four days after Marshall and I had begun our latest journey, I realized that this had been our longest trip to date. Also, we had visited nine FOBs during that time and had been to some of the most remote places our boys were stationed at in Afghanistan. I also realized that I was really tired.

This realization must have resonated on my face, because the first person to greet me with a welcome back embrace was my battalion commander, LTC Maranian. He could probably tell that I was wiped out, because he looked me in straight in the eyes and said, "Chaplain, you're not going anywhere for a while, OK? You look like you could use a break."

I didn't argue with him because I knew he was right. Besides, that Sunday was the start of the Advent season, and I was looking forward to being at my home FOB over the holidays. By December, winter had come on with a vengeance in Afghanistan. Temperatures dropped below freezing, and it became increasingly difficult to catch a Chinook out of Kalagush, so it seemed that God confirmed what LTC Maranian had said — I wasn't going anywhere for a while!

Chapter Twelve

New Year, New Chapel, New Beginnings

"If anyone is in Christ, he is a new creation, the old has gone, the new has come!" (2 Corinthians 5:17)

December 25, 2007, I wrote the following email to friends and family:

Dear Friends,

It's Christmas night here. While the day for most of you is just beginning, ours is coming to a close. And for most of us, this has been a day to remember all that we treasure in our lives. During our Christmas Eve service, we sang familiar Christmas Carols, read the Christmas story, broke bread together and sang Silent Night by candlelight. It was simple in its traditions, yet powerful in its message. For some, it was too much, and so they opted not to come. There's the Navy Reserve Chief who is a mother of four whose favorite tradition is celebrating midnight mass with her family. When I saw her this morning, she said that she couldn't make it to the service because she wouldn't have made it through the service. There's the Corps of Engineers civilian who works on improving our quality of life on the FOB. This is his fifth Christmas in a row away from his family. Three in Iraq, one serving on the Mississippi coast after

Hurricane Katrina, and now here in Afghanistan. I stopped to talk with him at the shower tent this morning. He's hoping this will be the last one for a while.

But then there were those who did show up last night. There's the young female MP, SPC Gray, who showed up unexpectedly. Last August, she came to talk to me after SGT Harris died. She wanted to be assured that she would go to heaven. I shared with her what God did for us through His Son Jesus Christ on the cross, and we prayed together for her to receive Him as her savior. But she's always been a little leery about coming to church. "Too many bad experiences with church, sir," she would always tell me each time I invited her. But last night she showed up. She sang along with all of the familiar Christmas Carols. She listened intently to the sermon, she came up to partake of the Lord's Supper. Afterwards, she told me that it was her first Communion. What better way to celebrate it than on the day of the Lord's birth!

Last night, by God's grace, we had a packed house. No surprise, as many tend to show up on Christmas and Easter. What was surprising, though, was that no one seemed to want to leave. After we had sung the last verse of Silent Night, most just stood at their seat. No one blew out their candles, or made their way to the door. Even after I had gone to the back of the chapel (or, conference room as it were) most just stood in the silence as if wishing it would continue. Gradually, one by one, they started to make their way out into the night. It was a full moon, so the night sky was as bright as I had ever remembered it on Christmas Eve. I wished each of them a Merry Christmas with a hug and a smile. When all of the Soldiers had left, Marshall and I put the conference room back together, wished each other a Merry Christmas, and then headed back to our rooms. Still lingering in the back of my mind, however, was that moment at the end of the service. What was it about that time that made it so sacred?

It didn't really hit me until tonight. Once all of the festivities of the day had come to a close, and all of the Soldiers had emailed, phoned or chatted online with their families and friends. After every Soldier had enjoyed a wonderful Christmas dinner where all of the officers served on the serving line, and It's a Wonderful Life had finished playing on AFN,

I realized what it was – for a brief moment last night, the sacred came down to touch each Soldier. The holy kissed them to make them feel whole when so many felt empty inside.

I imagine most on the FOB will never really be able to pinpoint what it was that they felt this past Christmas Eve at FOB Kalagush in Afghanistan. Most won't realize that it was God who placed them here, far away from all that they know and love. To place them in this wilderness away from all the distractions they face at home in order to remind them about what really is important at Christmastime. That, even though we are far from our families and the ones we love, they are not far from us. And even though we are fighting in a war that takes us far from home, home is never far from us. For the Prince of Peace who is able to give us the peace that passes understanding, and the God of Love who lavished us with His extravagant love by becoming a part of His creation in order that we might become children of God is, and always will be, Immanuel, God with Us.

May God bring you many blessings this Christmas, and may you rejoice that our God is with us,
Chaplain Don

New Year

The beginning of January saw Bagram receive six to eight inches of wet, heavy snow which shut down aviation assets for the better part of a week. I happened to be in Bagram to welcome in a new battery of Soldiers from Fort Bragg when the storm hit, so I was effectively stuck there for ten days. The sad part about it is that I had only planned to be there for five, which made for a lack of clothes towards the end. (Note to self – during the winter months, if you plan to be gone a week, pack for two just in case!) These guys were going to be a part of the battalion for the rest of the deployment as division has decided that we need more artillery assets in theater. They were brought into theater to field the Army's newest Artillery piece – the M777 Howitzer.

While both artillery pieces fire 155mm projectiles, the M777 is smaller and forty percent lighter (at just under 4,100 kg) than the M198 our battalion was currently using in theater. I also learned from one of our first sergeants, 1SG Frank Leudtke of Bravo Battery, that most of the weight reduction is due to the use of titanium. The lighter weight and smaller size allows the M777 to be transported by CH-47 (Chinook) helicopter or truck with ease, so that it can be moved in and out of the battlefield more quickly than the M198. The smaller size also improves storage and transport efficiency in military warehouses and Air/Naval Transport. What's more, the gun crew required is an Operational Minimum of five, compared to a previous size of nine.

Needless to say, having our Artillery brothers from the 18th Fires Brigade, XVIII Airborne Corps, join the fight would definitely help our Soldiers on the battlefield! So, seeing as I was their "defacto chaplain" it was great to be able to stand on the runway as they got off the plane to welcome them into theater. I think they enjoyed the fact that when I shook each of their hands, I put a phone card in it and said, "Call home as soon as you get a chance." What a blessing to be able to use the "Cell Phones for Soldiers" phone cards in my ministry!

So the New Year brought some new faces to the battalion and to our theater of operations. It also brought a lot of snow, as anyone from our platoon up in Lybert could tell you. During the storm that hit Bagram, the higher elevations received considerably more. Lybert was blanketed in over four feet! In talking with CPT Adam King, the platoon leader at Lybert who was in Bagram getting ready to go on leave, he said that his Soldiers were definitely making the best of the situation by sledding down the mountain on the mess hall's cookie sheets! I pictured Clark Griswold in *Christmas Vacation* careening down the mountain on a sled caked with cooking spray. I prayed that our guys didn't go so far down the mountain that they sledded right into Pakistan!

New Chapel

Perhaps one of the best new things to happen in the beginning of 2008 for our ministry here was the building of our new chapel at FOB Kalagush. After eight months of borrowing other areas to conduct worship services, complete with setting up and tearing down every week, we finally had a dedicated chapel! It was a wonderful addition to the FOB, as many came up to me to say how great it was going to be to have a place where we could worship, pray, and spend some quiet time with the Lord.

One of the best things about the chapel was the fact that there was going to be an office where I could finally give some private counseling, as well as a fellowship room complete with two morale phones, lounge chairs, books, devotionals, and coffee. On one wall we set up all of the children's books people sent in on bookshelves so Soldiers could come in, pick up a book and we could record them reading it in a warm and friendly setting. We then would send the recording to their families so the Soldier's children would see their parents reading them a book at bedtime.

As I looked at the local Afghan workers finishing the chapel, I remember being at Missoula Alliance Church in Missoula, Montana hearing our missionaries in China talk about the central significance of a church in their community. I was never able to fully appreciate what they were talking about until seeing our little chapel being built in the center of the FOB. It became a wonderful place for worship and for fellowship.

We dedicated the chapel in honor of SGT Taureen Harris who had died the previous August. In a moving ceremony both commanders, LTC Maranian and Commander Paparo attributed the building of the chapel with everything that was right with our armed forces. The 4-319th AFAR and the Provincial Reconstruction Team despite being different units, from different parts of the world, comprised of every branch of the military, had become a family at Kalagush and all of us knew it.

Hence, for the rest of our time in Afghanistan, Harris Chapel became a place where we could fellowship and show movies on Friday nights, hold Bible studies without having to compete with Soldiers watching TV in the dining hall, and a sanctuary where Soldiers could slip in to "take a knee" and allow the Lord to comfort them as warriors.

New Life

But I would be remiss if I didn't end this chapter describing the New Year without telling you about the best "new thing" of 2008. It's the story of Navy Petty Officer Cook and her new life with Christ.

Tokachena (pronounced Toe-kah-chee-nah) Cook is one of the RTOs in our operations center. Because of her zest for life, she had been nicknamed "Happy" by most everyone on the FOB. (I suspect it also had something to do with the fact that most of us didn't know how to pronounce Tokachena!) As a young girl growing up, she had had some bad experiences both with church and with Christianity. While not an excuse for turning away, it was an opportunity for her to decide what she really believed about spiritual things. But, as she tells it, one thing was sure — she did not want to have anything to do with Christianity.

Nevertheless, she didn't shy away from talking about her spiritual quest and her desire to know what was really the truth in religion. As a result, she found it quite easy to talk with my chaplain assistant, SPC Marcus Marshall. Marcus had a way of sitting down with someone, and just by his personality, drawing people into a warm and inviting conversation. He never judged anybody, and was always a gracious listener. (Even as I write this, I am again so grateful that the Lord had blessed me with such a great man to be my partner on our unit ministry team). So day by day, while Marshall would be working for the Mayor's Cell escorting local nationals onto the FOB, or guarding them as they worked on building B-Huts, Cook would often come and

sit with him before her shift. Somewhere during those conversations, Marshall invited her to check out our chapel service.
She promised that one day she would. A few weeks later, she
came to our contemporary service. She sat in the back, telling
me that she was just there to observe. I told her that she was
welcome anytime — even if it meant she watched from the
back. Because while I didn't know if she would respond, I did
know that she would at least hear the gospel.

At the end of the service, she came up to me with tears in
her eyes.

"Sir," she said smiling, "That was one of the nicest services
I have ever been to. I know that Marshall has told you about
my desire to figure out what I believe about God, and I'm glad
that I could come today."

I put my arm around her and said, "Happy, you are welcome here each and every Sunday. And I'll be praying that God
will get ahold of your heart."

However, aside from seeing Happy around the FOB, she
never did come back to chapel. But each time I saw her, I
prayed that God would get ahold of her life. Three months
later, that's exactly what happened.

In the beginning of December, Happy came back off
of her R&R leave. Marshall told me that she had something
exciting to tell me. So the next morning, I walked up to her as
she was leaving the dining facility. Seeing me, she ran up to me
and gave me a huge hug.

"Oh, sir!" she exclaimed. "I've been wanting to tell you
what happened on leave for me! I've given my life to Jesus
Christ!" I hugged her again and asked her to tell me the whole
story.

While she was on leave, she met up with an old high school
friend. Over dinner, Happy told her about her desire to know
the real truth about God, and how she had been checking out
all of the different religions. Her friend asked if Happy would

like to go to her church sometime. Happy told her that she would definitely come before her leave was over.

"Now, sir," she said with gleam in her eyes. "I'm a person of my word. If I tell you I am going to be somewhere, then I am going to be there. So on the last Sunday before coming back here, I went to church with her. But I have to be honest with you, I was only going because I promised I would."

And that's when it happened. In a little church in Maryland, Tokachena Cook again heard the gospel message and, this time, believed in her heart that Jesus was Lord.

"Sir, I had always said that I was not going to get married until I found the man who would satisfy all of my needs," she explained.

Then with wide eyes and a huge smile, she said, "And do you know what the pastor said that Sunday? He said during his invitation, 'If you have been looking all these years for the One who can satisfy all your needs, then you can find Him in Jesus. He is the One who will satisfy ALL of your needs!'" she exclaimed with her arms wide open.

"Chaplain," she said getting choked up. "It seemed like that pastor was speaking right to my heart. So I went forward that day to make Jesus my Lord and Savior!"

Well, by this time, *I* was crying! Once again, the Lord had shown me His masterful plan of calling one of His children home. Just as we read in the Scriptures, "I planted, Apollos watered, but God made it grow" (1 Corinthians 3:6), Marshall had planted the seed in inviting Happy to chapel, I had watered it by preaching a gospel message, but God brought it to true growth in her life through the nurturing of others.

As if this wasn't the best way to start out the Advent season, Happy had one other thing to share.

"Sir, the church where I received Christ was encouraging me to get baptized that day as a sign of my new life with Christ," she explained with a matter-of-fact tone to her voice. Then placing her hands on her hips she said, "But I didn't know any of those people! I know that the pastor was the one who preached the Word that led me to finally believe, but he was still a stranger to me. So I told them that I wanted **my** pastor to baptize me."

I guess I must have looked kind of dumbfounded when she said that because she pointed at me and exclaimed, "**You, sir! You** are my pastor! I would very much like it if you would baptize me in front of all my friends on this FOB."

Again, with tears in my eyes, I gave her a huge hug and told her that I would be honored to baptize her. The plan was to do it on her birthday — December 27, 2007. That way she could celebrate both her physical birthday as well as her spiritual one.

There was only one problem, though. We didn't have a baptismal! There was the river down below the FOB, but that was going to be logistically impossible, not to mention freezing. Still, Marshall and I wanted to be able to do this for Cook, so we asked our resident carpenter, Petty Officer Del Torro (affectionately known as "D.T.") if he thought he could build us one. He set to work on it right away in his spare time, and built a wonderful baptismal. While it was being built, Soldiers would come up to D.T. to ask if he was building a hot tub for the FOB. When he told them it was for a baptism, most thought it was awesome, and looked forward to being there on the day that Happy got baptized.

So on December 27, 2007, in front of all of her friends with whom she has been in combat, Tokachena Cook was baptized in the name of the Father, and of the Son and of the Holy Spirit, giving great testimony to the fact that even in a place like Afghanistan, God changes lives!

New year, new chapel, new life – all new beginnings. That's what all of us want at the start of each New Year. My prayer for 2008 was that the year would bring an end to these conflicts and the beginning of peace. My prayer was that as our battalion starts to wind down with its mid-tour leave for Soldiers, we would begin to see the light at the end of the tunnel for this deployment. I prayed that those who had not taken the time to think about eternal things would begin to this year. And I prayed that this would be the beginning of Jesus' promise of life to the full for all who seek it.

A glorious day! Toekacheena (Happy's) baptism. Chief Del Toro had to build me a baptismal. Most of the Soldiers thought it was a hot tub!

Chapter Thirteen

Red Cross Beatitudes

"Blessed is the one who does not fall away on account of me."
(Luke 7:19)

In this day and age of instant communication, it seems odd that the military still uses Red Cross Messages as their official notification system for Soldiers and their families whenever there is an emergency during times of war. What began as Morse code back in World War II has now been streamlined to email notifications, usually no more than three lines, stating the five W's (who, what, when, where, why), across official channels. It's how spouses and family members back home are notified if their Soldier has been injured or killed, and it's how Soldiers on the frontlines are told of an emergency back home.

One thing I learned early on in the deployment is that there always seems to be this unwritten belief that bad things are not supposed to happen to our families back "where it is safe." If tragedies occur, they should occur over here. While I remained grateful to the Lord that we hadn't lost any of our Soldiers at the hands of the enemy to date, we had definitely had our fair share of Red Cross messages resulting in Soldiers having to go home on emergency leave, and, in a way, they have still been casualties of this war.

On Good Friday, March 21, 2008, I had to deliver yet another Red Cross message to a Soldier. Shortly after our Good Friday service, the HHB commander found me to let me know that the father of one of our MPs had died. As with the majority of these messages in an oversaturated technological age, the Soldier already knew, but no official action could be done on the Soldier's behalf until an official Red Cross message is delivered. Consequently, as per protocol, I delivered the message and sat with her as she cried on my shoulder telling me how her father had died of liver cancer. Most of the time, I just sat and cried with them or held them in silence. One truth always remains, however — no matter what rank they hold, Red Cross messages do not discriminate.

After I left the Soldier's room, having made sure that her "battle buddies" would take care of getting her packed and ready for the flight the next morning from Kalagush, I walked outside and headed back to the chapel to pray. The moon was full that night. I stared up at it, trying to make sense of what often seems senseless in a combat zone. Over the course of the deployment, I had to hand out almost a dozen Red Cross messages for various emergencies back home. None of them were easy, but each of them was a blessed opportunity for ministry.

Blessed Are the Poor in Spirit

I don't think I will ever forget the first Red Cross message I had to deliver. I had been at Kalagush all of twenty-four hours. The Battalion Executive Officer (XO) pulled me aside to tell me that one of the Soldiers had a Red Cross message informing him that his twin brother had died two days earlier. When I asked why the Red Cross message hadn't been delivered earlier, the XO said, "Because his mother wanted to ensure that a chaplain was present to deliver it. We were going to deliver it anyway, but then we found you were coming in, so we waited. And now you are here."

Taking the message from the XO, I started my walk across the FOB to where the Soldier lived, praying that God would give me the right words to say. My friend and fellow chaplain, CH (CPT) Brian Koyn, gave me some of the best advice I could have received prior to going into a combat zone as a brand new chaplain. He wrote, "Always follow your gut — it usually isn't wrong when it comes to ministering to Soldiers."

SGT Malone was one of those guys who always had a smile on his face. Always laughing or cracking a joke, he never missed a chapel service. The day before, I had met him in the chow hall and he had told me how much he was looking forward to coming to chapel on a regular basis now that there was a chaplain on base. A happy-go-lucky guy, he truly wore his emotions on his sleeve.

When I caught him coming out of his B-Hut, I put my arm around him and asked if there were somewhere we could talk. We walked over to the smoking area and sat. Rather than simply hand the message to SGT Malone, I sat next to him and told him of his brother passing away. SGT Malone crumpled to the ground and sobbed. Kneeling down alongside him, he reached up and held on to me crying, "He was my best friend, sir. He was my best friend."

Within hours, we had SGT Malone on a flight home to Washington State. He would return to Afghanistan a couple weeks later. Over the course of a couple months, I would ask how he was doing, and while he didn't laugh as much anymore, there was still a sparkle in his eye and a constant dedication to the mission. He still did his job to the best of his ability.

"It's what my brother would have wanted," he'd say. "He couldn't join the military, but it was like he had joined because his twin brother was a Soldier."

Through his time of grief, he had learned who he was, accepted who he was, and tried to be himself — always to the glory of God.

"Blessed are the poor in spirit, for theirs is the kingdom of heaven." (Matthew 5:3)

Blessed Are Those Who Mourn

Perhaps worse than having to tell a Soldier that a loved one has passed away, is having to tell a Soldier that their young wife has suffered a miscarriage. As men, we always feel the need to fix things. We want to make things right. But when a Soldier's wife loses a baby prematurely, there's really nothing they can fix. Helplessly they go home on emergency leave to be with their grieving wife, not knowing what they can do to make it better.

That was the case with one of our young Soldiers on the gunline at Kalagush. SPC Grande was a Soldier from the backwoods of Tennessee, and he always had a quick one-liner that would crack up the entire Howitzer section. Several times when I sat with him at dinner he would have me in stitches talking about playing armadillo soccer or going frog giggin' down at the pond behind his house. He would often spout off, tongue-in-cheek, how his wife was spending all of his money "makin' the house look pretty" and how he just knew his wife was going to buy all frilly stuff for the baby's room, while he would have nothing to say in the matter because he was deployed.

A couple of times I would pull him aside and make sure he was really joking about that stuff and he would just smile and say, "Shoot sir! My wife is the best thing that ever happened to me. She's what brings a smile to my face every day!"

So it was a painful time for me the day that I had to tell him that his wife had miscarried fifteen weeks into her pregnancy. The often-joking young specialist was reduced to tears, but set about packing immediately to go home. I spent time helping him pack, mostly without saying a word.

"Sir, do you mind if I ask you a question?" he asked folding up a t-shirt to put in his ruck sack.

"Of course not, man." I said reassuringly.

"What do I do, chaplain?" he asked. "I mean, what am I supposed to do when I get home? There's no funeral. No arrangements to be made. I'm going home simply to be with my wife in a quiet house. What am I supposed to do?"

"You don't have to do anything, my friend," I said putting my hand on his shoulder and looking him in the eyes. "You just need to be there, and let your wife mourn. Mourn together."

He shrugged. "I don't reckon I know how to do that just yet."

"I know, son. But when you do, just know that this is how God heals us after a tragedy."

I remember praying with him — just before the Chinook helicopter came to pick him up — that God would be with him from the moment he stepped on the bird until he returned to the same spot, and that God would comfort him and his wife.

My prayers were answered almost immediately when I found out how quickly this young specialist got back to Germany from Afghanistan. When a Soldier has to go home on emergency leave, they are top priority for flights, and it just so happened that all the flights were aligned for him to get home. He was home with his wife in less than ten hours.

Later on, he would tell me how much of a blessing it was for him and his wife to be together. Our Family Readiness Group helped them by providing meals to running errands for them. They were even able to get away for a few days together. Their mourning eventually turned into dancing (Psalm 30:11)

"Blessed are those who mourn, for they shall be comforted." (Matthew 5:4)

Blessed Are Those Who Hunger and Thirst for Righteousness

One of the wonderful things that I was able to do on this deployment was meet one-on-one with Soldiers. There have been a handful of men that I met with on a regular basis. One Soldier and I were going through Jerry Bridges' *The Pursuit of Holiness*. Another was reading Steve Farrar's *Point Man* with me. Still another and I read John Eldridge's *Wild at Heart* together. Having grown up spiritually in the Navigators at West Point, I absolutely love one-on-one discipleship.

But it was a Red Cross message that brought SPC Wylie Turner and me together. Back in November, SPC Turner received a Red Cross message that his father was dying. Years ago, his father had received a double kidney transplant. For a time, both kidneys worked well. However, a few years ago one of the kidneys started to fail and he had to go back on dialysis. Major complications caused his other kidney to fail. He was retaining massive amounts of fluids and the doctors didn't seem too hopeful about his recovery.

The Red Cross message came through requesting Wylie come home ASAP. It was unsure whether or not he would even make it home to say goodbye. When I went to Wylie's room, he was beginning to pack. I asked if we could sit down and talk. Older than most specialists, Wylie was wise beyond his years. Before joining the Army, he had been through a lot, and tried his hand at just about everything when it came to employment. However, it wasn't until he and his wife had had their first child that he decided he needed a little bit more stability for his family. So he enlisted. While it did provide good housing and health care, deployment had its challenges for his little family.

He told me about his mother and father and how they had defied the odds as a young couple. Marrying when his mother was only fifteen and his father was seventeen, they had been happily married for thirty-eight years. His father was only fifty-five. After he told me about how serious his father's condition was, all we could do was pray. Wylie and I got down on our knees in his little room and cried out to God that He would at least allow Wylie to get home in time to see his dad. Moreover, we prayed that God would work a miracle in his father's life and bring him back to health again.

When we were done, Wylie got up and said, "Wow, sir. That's the longest I think I've ever prayed before. I hope God answers it!" I hoped so, too.

Throughout the weeks when Wylie was home, God worked a miracle in his father's life. Not only did Wylie make it home to see his dad, he also got to see his dad recover. The doctors were able to remove the bad kidney and, once they did, found that it was the root cause for the other kidney's malfunction. As we know, people can live normal lives with just one kidney, and it would seem that was going to be the case with Wylie's dad. When he returned to the FOB, Wylie told me the whole story. What a praise to our God as the great Physician and Healer!

That same week he came up to me and asked if we could start meeting together one-on-one. "I want to know God the way you know him, sir!" He said with great enthusiasm. "That prayer changed my life, and I want to know the power of Christ like you do!"

"Blessed are those who hunger and thirst for righteousness, for they shall be satisfied." (Matthew 5:6)

Blessed Are the Peacemakers

"Chaplain, is that you?" the XO asked shining his red lens flashlight my way. The new moon was up so there were times when you couldn't see your hand in front of your face just to walk to the latrine.

I had just finished an evening service and was headed back to my room. "It's me, sir, what's up?" I asked.

"We had a Red Cross message come in for one of the MPs. SPC Buzzard's dad died and she's asked to see you."

SPC Buzzard lives in Missouri. Over the past year I had really come to love this young woman. Although not a Christian, she took care of her fellow MPs and her family back home with incredible love. She always was telling me stories about her mom and dad and how she sent money home to help them when times were tough. Her big plans were to get out of the Army next year and open up a bar in her hometown. While many would cringe at the thought, I remember Tony Campolo was once quoted as saying, "More people are looking for Christ in bars and brothels than they are in church."

That week, the MPs had gone down to a small town south of Kalagush called Allingar. They were staying in the Provincial District Center there training new Afghan Police forces. Although not far away by convoy, we still needed to travel down there to pick up SPC Buzzard and bring her back to Kalagush to get her on a helicopter to send her out on emergency leave. After calling her squad leader on the cell phone (the only communication we had with them from Kalagush), the plan was to spin up the QRF and have me travel down with them to pick her up.

Only a few months earlier, I had travelled with the MPs to do a little humanitarian mission of my own. Several churches had sent Beanie Babies to give to the children of Afghanistan. For me, it was an eye-opening experience. As I passed out the stuffed animals, throngs of children crowded around us! It was wonderful to see such happy faces amidst such impoverished conditions. I especially loved giving Beanie Babies to little girls as it always seemed like they were being pushed aside in this male-dominated culture.

Traveling in a convoy as a chaplain is actually pretty interesting. You see, all of the Soldiers in the convoy have headsets which allow them to talk to each other on the trip. However, even though the Humvee seats four, you have to take into account the gunner. Obviously, the gunner needs to communicate with the driver and the team leader in the vehicle. So, when there are four riding and one in the gunner's seat that leaves four headsets for five people. I much prefer for Marshall to have a headset than me, so most of the time I just put in my earplugs and diligently look out the window for any suspicious activity and pray — a lot!

Before we knew it, we were in downtown Allingar. Our vehicle stopped in the middle of the street right outside the wall of the district center. The streets were abuzz with activity. Bakers selling "foot bread," small vendors selling soda pop, weavers selling their rugs and blankets. School was already out for the day so children were playing in the streets while the elders watched them, sipping their Afghan tea. But everything seemed to stop when our convoy approached. All eyes turned towards the vehicles in the center of the town.

I looked over to the gate of the district center. A couple of the MPs were helping SPC Buzzard with her gear. When I saw her come out, I immediately got out of the vehicle and she met me on the street behind the vehicle. As soon as she saw me, her eyes welled up with tears, and I opened up my arms to embrace her. And there we stood, in the center of this little town in full "battle rattle," Kevlar helmets touching and me holding her head as she cried. I told her how sorry I was to hear her dad had died and that I was going to be with her the whole trip back and would be there to help with anything she needed. I bent down to pick up her assault pack and walked her over to her side of the vehicle.

As I walked back over to my door, wiping away tears from my eyes, I couldn't help but look around me at all the staring villagers. They had all stopped what they were doing to watch as two Soldiers embraced in the middle of their town. I wondered to myself what was going through their minds as they watched one American Soldier console another in their time of grief. Would it be any different for them if a member of their family had lost a loved one? What if, for that brief moment, all of us, Afghans and American Soldiers alike, realized that, deep down, we are all the same? Created in the image of God, we laugh, we cry, we live, we love, we rejoice and we mourn.

"Blessed are the peacemakers, for they shall be called the children of God." (Matthew 5:9)

Blessed Are Those Who do not Lose Heart

I would be remiss if I didn't share about the Red Cross message that hit closest to home for me. In March 2008, my father went through triple bypass surgery. Originally, he was going in for a routine catheterization to see how the arteries around his heart were doing. However, when the doctor went in to look, she found things to be much worse than she had originally suspected, and admitted him to the hospital right away. The next day, my dad went into surgery. I hadn't quite grasped the magnitude of the surgery until I received a Red Cross message from my brother:

"Daniel B. Williamson informs CH (CPT) Donald A. Williamson, that their father, Bruce Daniel Williamson, is scheduled to undergo emergency bypass surgery on or about 9 March 2008. Brother requests Servicemember to call hospital prior to surgery. Presence is not required at this time."

The bad things that aren't supposed to happen back home were now happening to me. As I prayed and asked our chapel family to pray, I recalled the words of John the Baptist when he was imprisoned. He sent his followers to ask Jesus, "Are you the one who was to come, or shall we look for another?" (Luke 7:19) John was now in prison with no hope of escaping and he was questioning his calling, and questioning if he had been serving the right One.

I think we all go through that at some point when things seem to be at their worst. Is God in the midst of this? Does He even care? Does God really know what He is doing when He takes away an unborn baby from a young couple, or a parent away from a child?

When I called the hospital, I was able to talk with my father right before he went into surgery. We prayed together, and cried together. He told me he was proud of me and assured me that he would be OK, and I felt a peace that he would come through it with flying colors (which he did, and is now as healthy as ever!)

Jesus simply replies, "Blessed is the one who does not fall away on account of me." (Luke 7:19)

Red Cross messages may be the bearer of bad news. Some may feel that they are a necessary evil in times of war. But I've come to find that behind every Red Cross message is an opportunity to truly show people who receive them, that there is a Sovereign God who loves them, and works "all things together for the good of those who love him who have been called according to His purpose." (Romans 8:28b)

Chapter Fourteen

Love Across the Miles

"Whenever you did this to the least of these my brothers, you did it to me" (Matthew 25:40)

On both ends of Rest and Recuperation (R&R) leave, Soldiers stay in what is known as the R&R tent. On the one side of the tents are those guys who are shipping out to go on R&R leave. It's no surprise that the Soldiers in that tent are very excited to go home. One Soldier is heading home to his wife and two-month old son that was born when he was over here. When I was there, I prayed with him that he would savor every moment with his young family. Another Soldier was going home to celebrate his ten-year anniversary. Yet another was heading home to surprise his sister on her wedding day. And of course, there are those Soldiers who have no plans at all. They just want to go and sleep in a nice warm bed, take a shower without having to wear shower shoes, and eat at great restaurants.

Perhaps the thing that I was reminded of the most when with all of these Soldiers in the R&R tent is how much they appreciate the things back home now that they are away from them.

"You know sir, when you are here in Afghanistan," one Soldier mused. "You never realize how much you take for granted. Even little things like having a choice of what to eat are a big deal!"

I smiled. "It kind of makes you thankful for what we have been blessed with as a nation doesn't it?"

"Definitely!" He said.

So that was my prayer for these Soldiers as we headed back home. I prayed that our time would bring times of refreshing for us and a time for them to look at how God has blessed them, and remember why we were fighting over here.

My R&R leave finally came nine months into the deployment. In February 2008, I came home for eighteen days to be with my family. Wanting to simply get away from everything and everyone, Sue planned a trip to Spain's Canary Islands for eight days. And it was exactly what I needed. Not wanting to do too much, we simply did one thing each day. We stayed in a three bedroom villa right on the beach, woke up late, maybe watched a movie. Then we got into our rental van and went to places like *Loro Parque* (their version of *Sea World*), or walked along the boardwalk, or simply built sand castles on the beach with my two younger daughters. But then, before you know it, I was heading back to the combat zone in Afghanistan.

It's hard to put into words how it feels to come back after such a wonderful break, spending every moment I could with my family. There's a part of me that wished I never had to leave again. Many wives call R&R leave the "teaser" because it is just long enough for the family to get used to having their Soldier home again, but short enough to remind us how impermanent it really is. I would often replay the joy on my girls' faces when I came off the plane and juxtapose it with their tears when I had to leave again, and my heart was torn.

But I'm confident that, as hard as it was for them, my family knew this is what God has called us to do. We are missionaries in every sense of the word. Therefore, for this season in our life as a family, my ministry had to take me far away from them, while their ministry remained in our neighborhood back home in Germany. There's my faithful wife, Sue, who ministers to so many wives in the neighborhood; inviting them over for coffee, or going to lunch with them. She listens to them when they are missing their husbands, and takes the kids for them when she sees they need a break. She is my true partner in ministry.

There's Rachel who is very much involved with our middle school youth program, *Club Beyond* (Young Life overseas). Before we arrived, the club had about ten kids in it. When I went with her one Thursday after school, I counted twenty-five — most of whom were kids she had invited.

My daughter Keziah is perhaps the most faithful friend I have ever known. When she becomes your friend, she is your friend for life. She's a great encourager — even to her dad. The morning after arriving in Kuwait, I went over to the latrine to shave. When I opened my toiletry kit, I saw a hand-written card folded neatly inside. The front had a red heart on it with "I love you Daddy" in big block letters. Inside it read, *"Dear Daddy, I love you. I already miss you. I hope you are okay. It's just five more months. I can't wait until you come home again. I will count every day. I love you forever. Love, Keziah XOXOXO."* Her card helped take away a bit of the sting of having to come back.

Abby is the one who takes all of life in — with great intensity! When she goes to the beach, she doesn't just want to dip her feet in the waves, she wants to swim! When she does gymnastics and acrobatics, she wants to be able to do all the tricks and stunts *right now!* She loves AWANA and church, and tells all of her friends about her friend Jesus like He was simply another friend of hers. On leave, when we were walking home from school one day, she asked, "Daddy, is everyone going to go to heaven?" Pretty deep theological question for a six-year old!

"I hope so, sweetheart," I said squeezing her hand.

"But they need to love Jesus, right?" she asked matter-of-factly.

"That's right honey."

"And that's why you have to go back to Afghanistan," she stated looking up at me as we walked along the sidewalk. "I mean, we want our Soldiers to know Jesus, right?"

I looked down at her, trying not to get choked up. "That's right, baby. That's what God has called me to do."

She smiled, "Then it's OK if you go back."

"*. . . and a little child shall lead them.*" *(Isaiah 11:6)*

But this picture of love across the miles wouldn't be complete if I didn't tell you about my eight-year old, Hannah. The last night before heading back, I was sitting at the dining room table making a list of all the things I needed to ensure I packed, and Hannah came down the stairs holding a small red party bag. (The kind used by those of us that are gift-wrapping challenged)

She placed it in my lap and said, "Daddy, I put together some toys that I don't really play with very much anymore. They're not broken or anything, I thought that you might be able to give them to some of the kids that come through the doctor's office at Kalagush."

I opened up the bag. In it, she had put a blue Care Bear, a ball, and some plastic animals. I pulled her close to me.

"Thank you, sweetheart," I said, kissing her on the forehead. "I know that some little girl will cherish these toys. And she will love them even more knowing that they came from you."

So when I returned to FOB Kalagush that week, I unpacked my stuff and went over to the aid station to drop off the toys. Doc Ashby took them from me and said that he was sure there would be a little girl that came through who would love to get them.

On Sunday after chapel, the Doc invited me to the aid station to give me a picture. It was a picture of a little girl named Shameera. She was what many of our medics call, a "frequent flyer." Suffering from acute asthma, her parents had nowhere else to turn, and a year ago had seen her almost die from an asthma attack. Someone from their village had said they should try going to the American Army base for help. She'd been coming now for almost a year. Our female medic, PFC Knickerbocker, said that she would always light up the room when she walked through the door with her infectious smile. She appreciates everything that we do for her. So the medics didn't have to think twice about whom to give Hannah's bag of gifts. And when I told the medics the story about Hannah and her heart's desire to give her toys to a little girl that she may never meet this side of heaven, it touched their hearts as well.

"Mark this: Unless you accept God's kingdom in the simplicity of a child, you'll never get in." (Luke 18:17, MSG)

I think sometimes we forget the good things we are doing in Afghanistan. Even in the midst of battle, there can be peace. In the midst of sadness there can be joy. In the midst of crisis we can find hope. It may be by donating phone cards so Soldiers can call home, or it may be through websites like any-Soldier.com or americasupportsyou.mil. It may be by sending a care package to a Soldier whom you'll never meet, or sending toys and books to a school in Iraq or Afghanistan. Whatever it is, my prayer is that we don't forget that all of us, in some way, can help make this world a better place.

My family restored hope for me the eighteen days that I was on leave. I know that the Lord has blessed me beyond measure, and as such, I am compelled to bring hopeful blessings to others — Soldiers and local nationals alike.

Even if that means giving a Care Bear to a little Afghan girl with a smile that lights up the room.

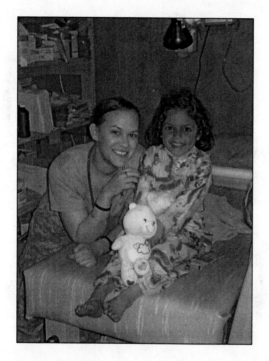

5-year old Shameera with our female medic PFC Knickerbocker.
This little girl was one of our "frequent flyers" at the aid station.

Chapter Fifteen

What Are You Doing Here, Chaplain?

"Consider Him who endured such opposition from sinful men,
so that you will not grow weary, and lose heart."
(Hebrews 12:2)

By April 2008, I truly needed a Word from the Lord. Moreover, I think that it is safe to say that I needed the Lord to give me a pretty good spiritual kick in the pants to keep me going. In late March, early April, we had to conduct our "Easter rotation." Over a ten-day time span, I would visit fourteen FOBs in order to give Easter chapel services to our Soldiers in the field. This became a priority and every chaplain was tasked to complete a grueling travel schedule, sometimes to places where we were being fired at even while on the choppers coming into the FOB. But no sooner had I just gotten back from Holy Week visits, I was being asked to go out once again.

One of my character flaws is that I am a person who thrives on structure. It doesn't have to be a dayplanner-all-planned-out kind of structure, but I find I am more at ease when I at least know in advance what I am about to do. However, by the end of April, that was not the case. So, needless to say, I was not in the best of moods prior to leaving. To put it bluntly, I was tired, frustrated, and in no mood to be the ambassador I should be to the Soldiers whom God had placed in my trust for whom to minister.

Just days prior, I had briefed the battalion commander that I believed our boys had hit the wall. We had all been here a year now, and we were tired — in every sense of the word. One Soldier probably put it best when he said, "I feel like an old weathered barn. I'm still standing, but it is probably only a matter of time before I fall."

To make matters worse, my time in counseling with Soldiers had, to say the least, been draining. It was like once we hit the one-year mark, the flood gates opened and problems abounded. A few of them help illustrate the severity:

- One Soldier learned that his wife of two years had been cheating on him the whole time they'd been married with two of his best friends from high school, and she's pretty sure that the two children they have are not his.
- Another returned back from leave only to find out that his wife is addicted to prescription pain killers and had depleted their entire savings and has begun procedures to put a second mortgage on their house.
- Still another found out that his wife had taken the kids and left their home in Ohio and he had no idea where she went. She said she needed to "find herself" and couldn't do that in Ohio. So with kids in tow, she got into her car and started driving. He hasn't heard from her in over a month.

In ministry, we are often told that when people come for counseling we shouldn't take their problems personally. We need to detach ourselves from them and simply allow them to vent, confess and seek comfort. That is easier said than done.

Maybe that's why I found myself drawn to the story of Elijah at the start of my trip. In 1 Kings 17-18, Elijah tells Ahab, the king of Israel, that, because of the nation's sinfulness, there would be no rain in the land until he said so. After three and a half years, there was a showdown between Elijah and the priests of Baal on Mt. Carmel to see who could make it rain. The priests of Baal went first and prayed to Baal to make it rain. For six hours they worked themselves into a frenzy — praying, chanting, and cutting themselves in order for their god to hear them. Nothing happened.

Then it was Elijah's turn. After literally soaking the wood so that it could not be lit by hand, Elijah prayed that God would burn up the wood and the sacrifice of bulls — and He did! It was an awesome victory for the God of Israel! Many came back to the Lord, and the false prophets were destroyed. After that, he prayed for the rain to come, and the Lord answered his prayer. After a three and a half year drought, God brought rain upon the Promised Land.

But then in what would seem to be a confusing reaction to his victory, Elijah retreated in fear. Threatened with execution by the queen, Elijah fled to a cave in the wilderness. Incredibly depressed, he even begged that the Lord would take his life, saying that he was the only one left who still followed God. Elijah's depression was great — so great even, that he forgot the incredible way in which the Lord had taken care of him during those three years of drought.

I can safely say now that I truly know how Elijah felt. The unit which I had called to be strong and courageous all this time, seemed to be waning in its resolve. With no apparent end in sight (or so it seemed to the Soldiers), they had been reduced to the here and now, forgetting all that God had brought them through to this point. What's more, many were finding that there was not much for them at home. Depression and exhaustion make for a dangerous combination in a combat zone.[2] And hearing day in and day out of our Soldiers' weariness, I found myself becoming depressed as well. Had God forgotten us? Had He brought us this far only to abandon us now? Would He remain faithful to His word that He would be with us wherever we go? In my heart, I knew it was still true, but in my head, I wasn't so sure.

Maybe that's why God met me in the pages of His Word that day. In 1 Kings 19, God told Elijah to stand at the mouth of the cave for He was going to speak to him. When Elijah had gone outside, a great and mighty wind tore through the mountains and broke the rocks, but the Lord was not in the wind. After the wind there was a violent earthquake, but the Lord was not in the earthquake. After the earthquake, there was a fire, but the Lord was not in the fire. Then came a soft, gentle whisper. And God was in the whisper.

"What are you doing here, Elijah?" the Lord said.

Elijah said, "I've been working my heart out for God, because the people of Israel have abandoned your covenant, destroyed your places of worship, and murdered your prophets. I'm the only one left, and now they're trying to kill me."

And gently, God reminded him that he wasn't the only one left, but that there were seven thousand who still followed Him. He told Elijah to get up and go back. God wasn't done with him yet.

I read that story one early morning in late April while sitting on a Hesco barrier at COP Fortress overlooking the

---

[2] In January 2009, the Army released that suicides reached its highest rate on record. The confirmed rate of suicides was 20.2 per 100,000 or 138 total in the Army. Army officials attributed multiple causes to why soldiers commited suicide, including long deployments, broken relationships, compounding legal troubles and financial problems.

But they were at a loss to explain why the suicide rate is going up. In the wake of these numbers, the Army ordered a servicewide "stand-down" for two to four hours of suicide prevention training.

Khorengal Valley. This valley had been the site of nearly all of our casualties in the brigade. Soldiers were killed fighting extremism and terrorism. Soldiers killed fighting for freedom. I thought about the wives and children they had left behind. I thought about my recent counselings with devastated Soldiers who may survive the war only to have no family to come home to when this is all over. I thought about all of that, and I was overwhelmed. I knew how Elijah felt.

Almost as if on cue, a warm breeze blew across my face.

"What are you doing here, chaplain?"

"I have worked my heart out in an effort to bring courage to the courageous," I replied. "But now as I sit here, I find that it could all be for naught. Soldiers are still dying while others have their families leaving them. Still others live with the consequences of sinful decisions they've made during this deployment. Am I the only one left?"

In a matter of seconds, God brought back to my memory everything He had done for our battalion to date. Tears streamed down my face as I remembered them. Just to name a few:

- The protection of our Soldiers on a convoy north of Kalagush.
- The faithfulness of strangers giving children's books for Soldiers to read at bed time.
- The construction of a chapel in the heart of the Muslim world.
- A dozen Soldiers coming to faith in Christ.
- The Boys of Bella.
- Cook's baptism.

And as if to put an exclamation point on the end of the list, I learned that day of God's miraculous hand on our platoon at Fortress.

The Soldiers of first platoon now residing at Fortress were only supposed to be there for a five-day mission. Task Force Rock was conducting a major operation in the Khorengal Valley, and they needed the gun support from our Howitzers. So, the Soldiers of first platoon packed up enough for a five-day mission, sling-loaded the Howitzers on Chinooks, and set up at Fortress in support of the infantry. That was six weeks ago.

Still, most of the platoon wasn't complaining very much. Oh sure, they hated the fact that they only had one uniform, and their X-box was up at Monti, but when I heard what happened at the beginning of April, I understand why Fortress was like a vacation for them.

The Miracle at Monti

COP Monti is similar in size to COP Bella. Barely large enough for one Chinook to land, it is surrounded on all sides by mountains. Once a very peaceful COP next to a small village, that all changed the moment the mullah told the commander at the COP that he could no longer guarantee the COP's protection. Around 1830 hours, one day early in April, just as folks were finishing their dinner chow, insurgents in the surrounding hills lit up the sky with rockets, RPGs, and small arms fire.

I sat down to talk with the Soldiers about what happened that night.

SGT Murphy was the first to speak. "Total chaos, sir," he said without emotion. "One minute we're sitting on our bunks in the B-Hut, and the next thing we know there are AK47 rounds coming in through the roof."

"I was sitting in the chow hall watching Sports Center when a round came and landed on my plate!" exclaimed SPC Harris. "I opened the door to the chow hall only to see tracer rounds zig-zagging across the sky. It was like watching a laser show."

Over the next half-hour, Soldiers sought cover anywhere they could find it. Near misses abounded. The battery first sergeant, 1SG Leutdke, attempted to make it over to the gun-line when an RPG whizzed by him just inches above his head. Fortunately for him, it didn't explode but simply bounced down the walkway like a rubber ball.

Gradually, either by low crawling or moving along B-Huts for cover and concealment, the boys made it to the Howitzers. Under a barrage of rocket and gunfire, these guys performed a direct lay of the gun in the vicinity of where the firing was coming. The infantry platoon at the COP got into their HUMVEES at the corners of the COP. Getting behind the 50-cal machine guns, they fired tracer rounds at the mountain. That was all the big guns needed. Like cannons on a warship, both M119 Howitzers fired ten rounds within a minute, lighting up the mountainside. And within a minute, all was quiet.

The Soldiers told me that once they had recovered and done an ammo and sensitive items check, they found, to their surprise, that there were no casualties. No injuries. Not even a splinter from rubbing up against the B-Hut for cover.

As I sat listening to this story, I'm sure I couldn't help but have an expression of utter amazement on my face.

So I simply asked, "Um, does anybody else here see this as a miracle?" Most of the Soldiers looked at me with bewildered faces.

Raising my hands and opening my eyes wide, I exclaimed, "You guys were in a fire fight for over thirty minutes, with what would appear to have been a surprise attack on the COP, and there were **no** injuries!"

"This is Joshua 1:9, guys!" I screamed. "God protected you through it all!" I pulled out my pocket New Testament with Psalms and Proverbs and read to them Psalm 91:4-8.

4 He will cover you with his feathers,
and under his wings you will find refuge;
his faithfulness will be your shield and rampart.
5 You will not fear the terror of night,

nor the arrow that flies by day,
⁶ nor the pestilence that stalks in the darkness,
nor the plague that destroys at midday.
⁷ A thousand may fall at your side,
ten thousand at your right hand,
but it will not come near you.
⁸ You will only observe with your eyes
and see the punishment of the wicked.

"Guys, arrows were flying all around you, and God protected you!" I proclaimed. "There's simply no other way to explain it than for it to be a miracle of the Lord."

The rest of the week at Fortress, we talked about the miracle. They could see what God had brought them through, and they knew that they could have hope for the future. Before Marshall and I left, we gave a gunline service on the same guns that were used to quell the storm at Monti. And I couldn't leave without a picture of first platoon overlooking that deadly valley. Some have coined it the Valley of the Shadow of Death. Maybe so, but I left believing that first platoon feared no evil for God was with them. (Psalm 23:4)

"What are you doing here, chaplain?"

I needed no further evidence from the Lord. When I got back to Kalagush, I put up my "life verse" as a chaplain onto my computer desktop. It read:

"My purpose is that they may be encouraged in heart and united in love, so that they may have the full riches of complete understanding, in order that they may know the mystery of God, namely, Christ, in whom are hidden all the treasures of wisdom and knowledge." (Colossians 2:2-3)

Twelve months and no casualties in the battalion. I prayed that night on my knees next to my cot. "Dear Lord, we pray you will faithfully bring all of us home safely, and that when we do get home, You will meet us there no matter what situations we face."

Though I am not a prophet nor the son of a prophet, I knew that I was to remain the Lord's servant to these Soldiers, and I appreciated the occasional spiritual kick in the pants whenever I need to be reminded of that.

The boys at Fortress. Only days before this picture was taken they survived what I called "the miracle at Monti"

Chapter Sixteen

Almost Home, and Yet . . .

"He who goes out weeping, bearing seed for sowing, shall come home with shouts of joy, bringing his sheaves with him"
(Psalm 126:6 ESV)

With a little more than two months to go, our Soldiers could finally see the light at the end of the tunnel. Morale was picking up. Soldiers were talking more and more with me about going home and the plans they had for their thirty days of block leave.

But war is a funny thing. You're never home until you can kiss your wife and kids and hold them in your arms again, knowing full well that you're not leaving anymore. And it doesn't matter whether you are one month into a deployment or one month from going home, the risks in a combat zone remain the same. The sting of that reality hit the 173rd Brigade hard, for nearly one quarter of the Soldiers killed in the brigade would occur in its last four weeks in country.

The black bracelet that would eventually adorn my right wrist was ordered on June 27, 2008, just three days after I learned that one of my friends, SPC Ryan Connolly, had been killed when his vehicle hit a mine on a routine patrol. With one in his vehicle already dead and others critically wounded, SPC

Connolly did not realize he had been severely injured and, as the platoon medic, he tended to all the wounded around him. The problem was, all his injuries were within, and before his unit knew it, he had bled out internally and died.

His death brought everything home for me because he was the first solder to be killed in this war that I could say I knew very well. A medic assigned to the 173rd Special Troops Battalion, SPC Connolly and I met on my many FOB "hops" to visit one of our gun platoons. Over the course of the deployment, Connolly and I would often get the chance to sit and talk together. And each time I held a field service at FOB Khogyani, Ryan was always there. I always looked forward to seeing him when I went there. But it wasn't until April of 2008 that I really got the chance to know Ryan in a very personal way.

That month, I was at Bagram again making my rounds to our many FOBs. This time, I was heading to the Pakistan border where one of our platoons had recently been given the mission of training Afghan borders and customs agents. As usual, I was stuck in an RSOI tent awaiting a flight. Ryan had just returned from his R&R leave and happened to get the cot right next to mine. Now, in an RSOI tent, there's not much to do. Some guys watch movies, others sleep, others read. Still others lie on their cots and "shoot the breeze." And that's what Ryan and I did for four days. And I learned a lot about SPC Ryan J. Connolly.

He told me that during his leave, he brought his young family home to Santa Rosa, California, to be with his parents. During that trip, he bought a 1970 Chevy Nova and began to restore it. He had a passion for baseball, classic muscle cars, NASCAR racing and all things mechanical.

I learned that he was able to be home for his baby daughter, Kayla's, one-year birthday. He shared with me how he and his wife, Stephi, could see that this deployment had started to take a toll on their marriage. But as he told me, "I'm going to do whatever it takes to make sure my marriage lasts, sir."

He loved his family, and he was excited that we would be having some marriage and family retreats after we got home. Over those four days, we became more than just medic and chaplain who served in the same brigade together. We became friends. And I will miss him very much.

Almost home, and yet . . .

In the beginning of July, my battalion commander, LTC Maranian, asked me to pack up my stuff at Kalagush and head to Bagram. With twenty-one days to go, Marshall and I went to Bagram Airfield to live in an RSOI tent that held over one hundred Soldiers as the battalion started to come through en route to home. Our battalion would eventually fly out on a total of five different flights, and LTC Maranian wanted me to be located in the theater's outbound tent to be amongst the rapidly redeploying Paratroopers. So as they came to spend anywhere from four to seven days in the tent, it became my responsibility to give them a redeployment brief, to listen, comfort, and help them get mentally prepared to reunite with their families back home.

Having packed everything out, all I had left was what could fit underneath my cot in the RSOI tent. But if there was one thing that I had learned over the last fifteen months, it's that there are times as a chaplain when you find ministry to do, and then there are times when ministry finds you. I experienced the latter in those last twenty-one days.

For much of the time during this deployment, when Soldiers weren't doing fire missions or on patrol, they were in their hooches watching movies or playing video games. It was how they escaped. That being said, now they were all in one big tent together, and I for one, was glad that they were. It's been said that the Soldiers who were the most well adjusted following combat headed home were those who fought in World War II. They didn't have any stress counselors or psychiatrists.

They weren't given reunion briefs or told about "battlemind" injuries. No, they just had each other, the stress of combat behind them, and twenty-one days to sit on their cots and talk about their experiences with one another. They talked about them on the train from Germany to France. They talked about them on their boat ride across the Atlantic. They talked about them while waiting in endless lines to out-process the Army.

Nowadays, we fly our Soldiers home and they can be out of a combat zone in less than forty-eight hours. But that doesn't give them much time to "de-program." So I found that having our Soldiers come to Bagram for at least a week before they go home turned out to be a good thing. They were in close quarters with their fellow Soldiers, and they had nothing to do put play cards and talk.

And that's where I and SPC Marshall came into the picture as a Unit Ministry Team. Our cots were smack dab in the middle of the tent. For much of the morning and evening, I would simply walk around the tent and talk to Soldiers. Many opened up about their experiences, some as recently as the week before when the engineer company that was stationed with our guys at FOB Khogyani lost SPC Connolly. These Soldiers got the chance to simply tell their story, and how his death affected them greatly.

Almost home, and yet . . .

Our greatest losses as a Brigade happened on July 13, 2008 in a little Combat Outpost near the village of Wanat in the Waygal Valley. The position was being defended primarily by 2nd Platoon, Chosen Company, 2nd Battalion, 503rd Infantry Regiment. On July 8th, the platoon began building a patrol base (COP) and separate observation post near Wanat with the mission of disrupting Taliban activity in the area. The base covered an area about three hundred meters long by one hundred meters wide. Lacking heavy equipment, the base was not strongly fortified, instead being protected by sandbags and barbed wire. An Afghan company contracted to help build the base's defenses failed to appear.

Soldiers at the base noticed warning signs in the local area, including groups of men watching the base construction from the nearby village and other groups of men moving through nearby mountains. At a dinner meeting in the village, a villager told the Americans that they should shoot any men seen moving through the nearby mountains and asked them if they were conducting drone surveillance around the nearby area.

On the evening of July 12th, Taliban Soldiers moved into Wanat and ordered the villagers to leave. The Taliban, unde-tected by the Americans, set-up firing positions inside houses and a mosque. Early on the morning of the 13th, Taliban forces fired on the base from the village using machine guns, RPGs and mortars exploiting homes, a bazaar, and a mosque in the village as cover. Another one hundred militants attacked the observation post from farmland to the east. When it was all over nearly four hours later, nine U.S. Soldiers were killed in the attack, mainly in the observation post. Between twenty-one and fifty-two militants were reported killed with another twenty to forty wounded, but coalition forces found only two Taliban bodies after the battle. The battle would go down as the highest death toll for American troops in Afghanistan since an operation known as *Operation Red Wing* occurred three years prior. Many of these Soldiers were men that I had met when I did ministry up at Bella back in November.

To say that this put a damper on our Soldiers' reunion plans was a gross understatement. It literally took the wind out of our sails. It was a bitter reminder that we were not home yet. All of us were supposed to be home in a few weeks. So many of my Soldiers in the artillery knew these guys. They fired for them whenever they were in contact. They all expressed how much they wish they could have been there. I felt the same way. How would I have ministered to these brave warriors? Unexpectedly, I was given that chance the very next morning.

I was standing in line for eggs when a young specialist came in the door to stand behind me. He was walking with one crutch. I asked him what he had done to his leg. He very quietly said, "Oh, I was injured in combat a couple of days ago."

Knowing what had just happened that week, I asked, "Were you one of the guys at Wanat?"

He nodded and said, "Yes, sir, I was one of the guys up on the OP when we got hit."

I put my hand my hand on his shoulder, trying real hard not to show too much emotion. I smiled and said, "You guys have had a rough go of it up there, haven't you?"

He smiled, nervously. "Yes, sir," he replied. "Chosen company has sure been hit hard this deployment." (From the ambush at Bella and now the battle at Wanat, Chosen Company by this time had lost fifteen Soldiers; fifteen out of a total of forty-two for the brigade)

So after we had gotten our eggs made to order, (a great luxury all of us look forward to whenever we come through Bagram!) this young Soldier and I sat down together for breakfast. In the thirty minutes we were together, I learned a lot about SPC Chris McKaig. I learned that he was from Oregon, that he loved to fish, and that he couldn't wait to get home to see his parents. I learned that he has a mother who worries a lot (but to be expected with all that has happened.) I learned that he loves his job, and he loves his company. But most of all, he loves his fellow Paratroopers. As he told me what happened up at the OP, his hands shook, describing the living hell he and the other eight Soldiers went through up on that hill for nearly four hours. He told me how the Taliban briefly breached the wire of the observation post before being driven out. And that after almost half an hour of intense fighting at the observation post he was the only Soldier who remained. Chris was the fortunate one.

"But you know sir," he said, tears welling up in his eyes. "I've learned that while I love my job, I really hate war."

"Son," I said in a choked-up voice, "I'd be worried if you didn't hate war."

He smiled and then said, "But the other thing I've learned is how much love I've felt since all this happened. Everybody has been so helpful, and so encouraging. Nurses, doctors, chaplains like yourself. Paratroopers coming over to the hospital to see how were all were doing. They really care, and that has helped."

At one point, I asked Chris if he had any type of faith. He said, "Well, it's funny you should ask that. You see, I didn't grow up in a religious home, but my grandmother was always going to church. And every chance she got, she would take me along. She'd always tell me, 'Chris, there's something different about you. I know that God has great plans for you, and that He will use you someday.' I guess this is what she meant."

I laughed and said, "Well praise God for godly grandmothers!"

"Yeah!" he replied, surprised. "Guess my guardian angel was working overtime a few days ago!"

Hal Moore, the battalion commander for 1st Battalion, 7th Cavalry which fought on LZ Xray in Vietnam, from which the book *We Were Soldiers Once . . . And Young* and the movie, *We Were Soldiers* is based, said this about why some of his men, including himself, were spared and others died.

"I can't tell you why a bullet hits one Soldier and doesn't hit another. But the fact that it doesn't, means that those who are left still living are meant for something else, something greater. There will come a day when we are all 'taken out of the game' and on that day, I will be, once again, reunited with my men."

I shared that with SPC McKaig as we got up from the table. I told him that the greatest gift he could give to those that were left behind here would be to serve with honor, and validate the sacrifice his brothers made for him up on that OP. We hugged and I watched as a great warrior, a hero, slowly walked out the door of the chow hall.

"Greater love has no man than this, that he lay down his life for his friends." (John 15:13)

Later that morning, that verse went through my head as if on continuous repeat while I stood at attention, holding my salute, standing on the side of road on Bagram Airfield as nine flag-draped coffins passed by me and the thousand other Soldiers who lined the street. There were no words to capture the moment. Only silence and sadness, and the reminder, once again, that we were not home yet.

The bitter reality in all of this was that, if all of our Soldiers made it to Bagram Airfield and then on to Bamberg in those next couple of weeks, the 4-319th Artillery would be the only battalion in the brigade that had not lost one Soldier on this deployment. And although this had been my prayer from the beginning, and I give God all the glory and praise, I found myself having mixed emotions. On the one hand, I praise God that He had protected all of the Soldiers in my flock, for we have not been without close calls. And yet, what of my other fellow chaplains? No doubt they prayed the same prayer for their battalion. In truth, I don't understand.

"There but for the grace of God, go I."

Thankfully, that prayer was answered. All of the Paratroopers of 4th Battalion, 319th Airborne Field Artillery Regiment made it home alive.

I pray that someday, all of the warriors I served with will be able to tell that story — how the God of Abraham, Isaac, and Jacob, in His extravagant love and grace, protected every one of us. How we were strong and courageous, because the Lord our God was with us wherever we went.

Ryan J. Connolly and his daughter, Kayla the day he headed back from his R&R, April 2008.

Epilogue

Ministering to Heroes

"I have fought the good fight, I have finished the race, I have kept the faith." (2 Timothy 4:7)

July 27, 2008

I read that verse this past Sunday in chapel in praise to the Lord for getting us through this deployment. Yesterday, the last of the Soldiers arrived back to Bamberg. Now the 4-319th Airborne Artillery Battalion is home. As I shared in chapel, our battalion was the only battalion which, miraculously, suffered no fatalities or battlefield injuries. And there were countless times when there could have been many. Of course, the only explanation for this is God's grace and answered prayers. I cannot express my gratitude enough for how much the prayers and support of families and friends have meant to me and to all of our Soldiers over these past fifteen months. They blessed us more than you could ever know, and for that I say, "Thank you."

As I looked over the sea of people in the gym yesterday — Soldiers hugging their family members with cameras rolling to catch every precious moment — I was struck by the reminder that even though this battle is over, the war is not — both the war on terror as well as the war for people's souls. While we may experience peace for a season, I'm reminded that there will be no lasting peace until the Prince of Peace returns. So until then, I will continue to run to the battle, wherever that takes me — be it on the battlefields Afghanistan, or the Warner Barracks in Bamberg, Germany. The calling to be a chaplain, the shepherd of warriors, is indeed an honor.

A couple of nights ago, I was putting my younger two daughters to bed. After telling them a story, and praying with them, I gave them each a kiss goodnight and rejoiced at being able to tell them I would see them in the morning. As I turned out the light and got ready to leave, my daughter Hannah stopped me in the doorway.

"Daddy," she asked, "Are you a hero?"

I turned around to face her. "No, baby. I'm just a chaplain," I smiled in reply with tears welling up in my eyes. "But God allowed me to minister to a whole battalion of heroes."

With that, I closed the door to their room…and to one of the greatest years of ministry I've ever had the privilege to experience.